The
Backyard
Traveler

The Backyard Traveler

by

RICHARD MORENO

Published by
The Carson City Children's Museum

1 9 9 1

To Hank, the smartest, most wonderful boy in the world.

Acknowledgements

THE CARSON CITY CHILDREN'S MUSEUM is very appreciative of all the efforts towards the publication of this fundraising project. We want to particularly thank Richard Moreno for writing this book, Paul Cirac of White Sage Studios for the design and production, Dale Wetenkamp, Don Ham, Lisa Tolda and Sandi Wright of the *Nevada Appeal* for the marketing, advertising and preparation of the photography, Jim Padgett and his crew at Silver State Industries for the printing, Jim Penrod of Printers Ink for the photographic screen, and all of the other people and organizations who have helped with their knowledge and advice.

Suzi Meehan

Fundraising Chair

Contents

CONTENTS

Preface:
A Museum for Children

THE PURPOSE of the Carson City Children's Museum is to establish a facility in Carson City that will provide a unique and innovative learning environment in Nevada, broadening horizons in the arts, humanities and sciences through enjoyable hands-on experiences.

With a 30-year lease for the historic Carson City Civic Auditorium signed, sealed and delivered, we have made real progress toward our goal — the establishment of a children's museum in Carson City.

Our most significant accomplishment in 1990 was the May 18 opening of "A Most Excellent Adventure . . . a sampling of hands-on exhibits for kids of all ages." Located in the Changing Gallery of the Nevada State Museum, this joint venture was designed by both members of the Children's Museum Exhibit committee and the exhibit staff of the Nevada State Museum.

For younger children, "Here is the Church, Here is the Steeple. . . " — designed by local artist Kathy Jordan — is an entertaining array of miniature doors, windows and latches which children can open to discover delightful cartoon surprises. The younger set can also "Make A Face" by sticking a selection of eyes, ears, noses and mouths onto a huge clown's face.

For older kids, State Museum staff used their own ideas and the Exploratorium Cookbook (a publication by San Francisco's Exploratorium with "recipes" explaining how to make many of its popular exhibits) to construct some fascinating exhibits.

Visitors can also test their reaction time with "Speed Trap," figure out the basics of electrical connections by putting together the electrical puzzles in "Current Events," leaving their shadow on a wall glowing with phosphorescence in the "Shadow Box," and disorient themselves by peeking into the "Incredible Shrinking Room." In one popular exhibit — an original designed by the State Museum staff — visitors pedal an exercise bicycle to turn on a television — accompanying text asks them to ponder energy use in their daily lives.

The centerpiece of the show is "Stuffee," a seven-foot-tall soft sculpture whose torso zips open to reveal stuffed kidneys, lungs, a heart and other organs. Docents give regular talks about physiology and Stuffee's insides. Visiting children particularly enjoy helping the docent to pull out Stuffee's 25-foot-long small intestine.

More than 75 Children's Museum volunteers, clocking over 1,500 hours, have guided in excess of 37,000 visitors through the exhibit in the first year, including over 200 school groups. The response has been overwhelmingly enthusiastic! In fact, the show was so successful that its run was extended to the end of 1991.

The Children's Museum has received generous support from the northern Nevada community for "A Most Excellent Adventure." Financial support came from Nevada Bell, First Interstate

Bank, the Truman Orr Foundation, Superscale International, the Carson City Convention and Visitors' Bureau and numerous individuals and businesses. Members of the Carson-Douglas Medical Auxiliary purchased Stuffee and donated him to the museum.

Along with the ongoing responsibility of running and maintaining "A Most Excellent Adventure," our efforts have been geared towards the capital campaign. Our first priority is to raise funds for the renovation of the Civic Auditorium.

Carson City's Civic Auditorium was built in 1939, a Works Project Administration project designed by Nevada architect W.A. Ferris. The red brick, Romanesque revival-style building anchors the north end of Carson City's downtown district. In 1990, it was placed on the National Register of Historic Places.

Originally used as an auditorium and community center, later as offices, the city-owned building has been empty since 1983. In November 1989, the Carson City Board of Supervisors voted to lease the building to the Children's Museum, and in September 1990, the lease was signed. The Children's Museum will pay token rent — $1 per year — for ten years, providing us time to complete building renovation and get the museum on its feet; after ten years rent will rise to market rate and the Children's Museum will have an option to buy the building. Its central location makes access convenient for both residents and tourists. It is close to Carson City's other attractions, only a block north of the Nevada State Museum and six blocks north of the State Capitol. Inside, the building measures approximately 15,000 square feet in a basement, mezzanine and main floor. There is space in the basement for offices, classrooms and exhibit construction shops. On the main floor, the spacious auditorium with its high ceiling, tall windows and wood floor will serve very well as exhibit space; a separate room near the entrance could hold a museum gift shop. An existing stage will be retained for youth productions.

The renovation will restore the building to its previous important role in the life of the community, thus bringing families downtown and helping to rejuvenate Carson City's downtown district.

Although well constructed and structurally sound, the Civic Auditorium is in need of extensive rehabilitation to meet current building code requirements.

An initial estimate puts the cost of the work at more than $300,000. The Children's Museum has hired an architect, Arthur Hannafin and Associates, to commence the architectural work. Mr. Hannafin has worked with the Children's Museum Board of Directors to define space needs and determine special requirements for exhibits.

He also has helped the museum to refine a detailed building renovation budget, for which we have received some sizable donations, including grants from the Carson City Convention and Visitors' Bureau, the Truman Orr Foundation, First Interstate Bank, Nevada Bell, the Grace Dangberg Foundation and Sierra Pacific Resources, Independence Mining Company, State Farm, E. L. Cord Foundation, Carson City Redevelopment Authority and the City of Carson City as well as support from IBM, the Carson-Douglas Medical Auxiliary and hundreds of individual donors.

The Carson City Children's Museum enjoyed a busy and successful year in 1990. On February 23, 1991, we opened a traveling exhibit, "Leonardo," at the Ormsby Public Library. This outstanding show included 25 hands-on replicas of Leonardo da Vinci's inventions.

We were pleased to have worked with the Ormsby Public Library on the "Leonardo" project. We look forward to bringing many more such shows to northern Nevada once the museum is established in its permanent facility.

Since incorporation in 1988, docent coordination and scheduling, publicity, planning, fund raising, grant writing and general management have been performed by volunteers. However, the museum has reached a point in its growth where professional, paid staff has become necessary. The work load has increased exponentially during the past year, and proper management will help assure the timely success of the project.

The Board of Directors has decided its top priorities for the coming year will be obtaining funding for two staff positions, renovation of the auditorium and construction of exhibits.

As we continue to offer a variety of educational exhibits for the public to enjoy, our capital campaign proceeds in earnest! The proceeds of this book have been generously donated by its author, Richard Moreno, to assist our efforts in making the Carson City Children's Museum a permanent part of Carson City.

Sincerely,

Jenny Kilpatrick
PRESIDENT,
BOARD OF DIRECTORS

Foreword

SOON AFTER Richard Moreno started writing his "Backyard Traveler" column for the *Nevada Appeal* several years ago, it became apparent that the columns would make a nice book.

They made interesting reading or Carson City-area residents and visitors alike. Each of them contained that spark of fun, excitement and curiosity that reflect Moreno's personality.

So in late 1990, after I agreed to help get a collection of "Backyard Traveler" columns published in book form, Moreno selected some of his best columns and started updating and editing them.

But by the time he brought the finished version to me on a computer disk, I still had not figured how to get his book published on a low budget.

I knew "Backyard Traveler" which had generated a lot of enthusiasm from *Appeal* readers, would be a great thing for Carson

City tourism, and a great thing for locals to have. Some very good travel books about Nevada had been published years ago, but there was nothing current and nothing extensive about places to visit in the Carson City area itself.

Then members of the Carson City Children's Museum board came to the *Appeal* for help in a fund-raiser. And suddenly, it all came together.

I knew that Moreno didn't want to accept any payment for his book, because some of it was researched while he was on the payroll of the Nevada Tourism Commission. And we had talked in the past of finding a good, local project which could benefit from the profits of "Backyard Traveler."

I made a quick call to our traveling writer, put him in touch with the Children's Museum board, and the book was on its way to reality.

Appeal publisher Dale Wetenkamp and I agreed to help the Children's Museum. We decided to handle it as a community service project, lending our publishing expertise and *Appeal* promotional support to the project. We even got Lisa J. Tolda, our staff photographer, to print the photographs that Moreno had taken of his visits, and screened the photos for publication.

It was difficult for the *Appeal's* editorial board — which consists of Wetenkamp and myself — to be anything but strongly supportive about the Children's Museum project. It was an exciting concept for our small town, a project that would not only educate our children about the world's mysteries, but also encourage tourism in the capital city. Moreno felt the same way.

But it was members of the Children's Museum board who did the real work. They arranged for the composition, art work and printing, all at a price within their small budget.

Readers will enjoy *Backyard Traveler,* the book. Even those who have clipped his columns from the *Appeal* will find this book handy to use for planning day trips in and around Carson

City, and the perfect gift for friends and relatives visiting the capital city. The book also features maps that make it easy to find your way on some of northern Nevada's back roads.

While reading *Backyard Traveler,* it's also nice to know that the profits from the book are going to a very good cause — toward the creation of the Carson City Children's Museum, a museum that will become a reality in just a few years.

Donald Ham
EDITOR
NEVADA APPEAL
Sept. 5, 1991

Introduction

WHO WOULD HAVE THOUGHT IT?

In early 1987, *Nevada Appeal* Editor Don Ham asked me if I was interested in writing a weekly column for the Sunday edition of his paper. He said he was looking for a travel column and thought I would be a good choice because of my job as public relations director for the Nevada Commission on Tourism.

I accepted and assumed it was something I could probably sustain for about a year or perhaps 18 months. I sat down and wrote out as many ideas for columns as I could — compiling about 30 — and wondered if I would even have enough material for a year. Fifty-two columns suddenly seemed like an awfully large number.

Well, Don must be a shrewd editor, because more than four years later I'm still churning them out and haven't yet run out of ideas. I've got to admit there have been a few tough spots where it certainly seemed like I'd finally reached the end of the line — but usually something would pop up and save me for another week.

Another big help have been the wonderful readers of *The Backyard Traveler*. At least a few of the ideas for columns originated with a telephone call from someone suggesting a place I'd never heard about or didn't know how to reach. Foremost among those has been Lois Lazar of Carson City, who has possibly seen every square inch of northwestern Nevada. She is a true Nevadaphile who loves exploring the history of this state.

Most of the research for the column was — and continues to be — done on weekend trips with my son, Hank. While he may only be a toddler, he has been a great traveling companion and, when called upon, makes a pretty good model for my photos.

In fact, photos have been one of the biggest challenges of doing the column. In my previous life as a newspaper reporter I was occasionally asked to take my own photos for a story but always knew that if I blew it the paper could send a photographer back to reshoot an assignment. No such luck with this column.

Fortunately, the *Nevada Appeal* is blessed with an extremely talented photographer, Lisa Tolda, who can take my film and turn it into useable photography. Despite the occasional bad lighting, thin negatives, bizarre composition and other quirks in my photos, she regularly turns my coal into, if not exactly diamonds, something akin to cubic zirconium.

Other good people at the *Nevada Appeal* who have made sure that it appears each week have been Michelle Quintero, my first editor there, and Sandi Wright, who continues to see that I don't misspell "ichthyosaur" or mistakenly put Pahrump in Pershing County.

Don Ham was the one who suggested turning "The Backyard Traveler" into a book. He said that readers enjoyed it and might like to have the columns compiled into a more permanent format.

Don approached the Carson City Children's Museum to propose publishing a *Backyard Traveler* book as a fundraiser. I liked the idea, wanting to contribute something back to the community, and the Children's Museum folks thought it just might work. They are courageous, wonderful people — so buy lots of copies for your friends, family, dog, cat, gerbil, etc.

The result is *The Backyard Traveler: The Book* (which will soon be followed by *The Backyard Traveler: The Movie, The Backyard Traveler: The TV Show, The Backyard Traveler: The Cartoon* and *The Backyard Traveler: The Coffee Mug*).

I have compiled what I consider the best of the 200 or so columns I've written over the past few years. I'm sure that others might select different choices but I feel the 54 columns contained within offer some of the best ideas for day trips in northern Nevada.

A few are a bit afield and might take more than a day to properly enjoy. Fortunately for me, Don Ham has never limited my vision and has generously allowed me to write about places all over Nevada. In this book I have, however, not included places that would be considered southern or far eastern Nevada. Perhaps if this book is well-received there will be a sequel that can include the rest of the state as well as those parts of northern California that have been the focus of my columns.

Like every person who writes something for a newspaper, I both love and hate doing it. Each week before my deadline I curse the day I agreed to write the darn thing. And each week, I get such a feeling of satisfaction when I pick up my Sunday paper and see my byline.

It's been a kick to write and I hope everyone has as much fun discovering the places mentioned here as I did writing about them.

Richard Moreno
AUGUST 1991

PART I

Around the Capital City

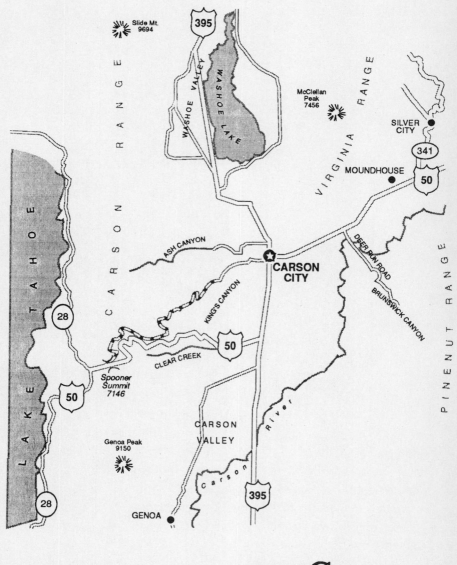

Slide Mt. 9694

395

Washoe Valley

Washoe Lake

McClellan Peak 7456

SILVER CITY

341

50

MOUNDHOUSE

VIRGINIA RANGE

ASH CANYON

CARSON CITY

DEER RUN ROAD

BRUNSWICK CANYON

PINENUT RANGE

LAKE TAHOE

28

KING'S CANYON

50

CLEAR CREEK

50

Spooner Summit 7146

CARSON VALLEY

Genoa Peak 9150

River

395

Carson

GENOA

28

Main Highway
Secondary Highway
Dirt Road
River or Stream
Area of Interest
U.S. Route Marker
Interstate Highway
State Highway

395

80

844

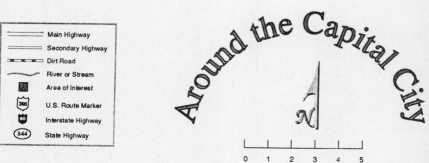

Around the Capital City

N

0 1 2 3 4 5

Around the Capital City

WHEN I FIRST MOVED to the Carson City area, a smart-mouthed journalist friend of mine from Southern California asked me what there was to do there. Not being completely familiar with the area, I told him it was a nice town that was only a half hour from Lake Tahoe and Reno, a couple of hours from Yosemite and about two hours from Sacramento.

He joked that Carson City should change its slogan to "Carson City — it's close to a lot of nice places."

The reality, of course, is that Carson City has perhaps more things to do and places to see than most communities its size. Partially as a result of its status as the State Capital, the town boasts an unusual number of attractions, such as the State Museum, the State Railroad Museum, a large historic district and the State Capitol.

Additionally, Carson City was there during the state's earliest years, playing an important role in the creation of Nevada, which provides it with a number of significant historic sites.

While most other early Nevada communities prospered because of the presence of gold and silver, Carson City developed as a crossroad community, serving as an important stop on the Pony Express and stagecoach routes and, later, connecting Virginia City to the world and housing the machinery of state government.

As a result, Carson City has survived while other communities, such as Virginia City, experienced the ups and downs associated with mining. And, unlike many Nevada towns, it has been able to keep most of its history in pretty good shape.

Its location on the east side of the Sierra Nevada has also blessed Carson City with some beautiful natural areas. Just beyond the neat rows of houses are picturesque canyons like Clear Creek, King's Canyon, Ash Canyon and the Carson River corridor.

The following are just a few of the places a real backyard traveler can explore in and about the Capital City.

Carson City's Majestic Historic Homes

THEY STAND ON QUIET STREETS shaded by large trees; in neighborhoods seemingly untouched by the years. They are Carson City's elegant ladies — the historic homes of the state's founders.

Located on the city's west side, in the area roughly bounded by Mountain Street, North Carson, Third Street and Washington Street (although there are other fine historic buildings outside of this area), these serene structures help tell the story of Nevada's early days.

The reason these stately homes exist is that in 1861, Carson City was designated the state capital — during the heyday of the fabulously rich Comstock Lode — and soon became home for many important mine owners, lumber magnates and railroad officials eager to be close to the political action.

While few remember the names of these early Nevada giants,

it is fortunate for us that many of their residences have survived into the 20th century and offer a fascinating glimpse into the lifestyles of the rich and famous of more than a century ago.

One of the best ways to learn about the historic district is to pick up a copy of the Carson City's Historic Tour brochure, available at the Carson City Chamber of Commerce.

For example, the brochure points out that the home at 311 W. Third Street was built in 1869 by agriculturalist George Washington Gale Ferris. Ferris is notable in Carson City's development because he imported from the east coast a large number of the trees planted throughout the city. However, of perhaps more interest is the fact that George Ferris' son was the inventor of the Ferris wheel and grew up in the house.

A drive through the historic district is a fun and interesting way to learn about the history of Nevada. For instance, the Bliss Mansion at 710 W. Robinson Street was built in 1879 by Lake Tahoe lumber and railroad magnate Duane L. Bliss. Bliss made his fortune with the Lake Tahoe Narrow Gauge Railroad that carried timber from Lake Tahoe to Virginia City's mines.

Of course, the Governor's Mansion, across Mountain Street from the Bliss home, is a worthy residence for the state's chief officer. Built in 1908 at a cost of $22,700, the Southern Colonial-style mansion has been home for 17 governors and their families and pets.

The two-story mansion incorporates four classic white columns at the entrance and a beautiful curved second-floor porch. Inside it boasts about a dozen rooms, including a large dining room and parlor, library and seven bedrooms.

A few houses down is the picturesque Niles-Sadler house at 310 N. Mountain Street, which was built in 1878 by Edward Niles, paymaster and general ticket agent for the V & T Railroad. The home was purchased in 1896 by Governor Reinhold Sadler and was considered the unofficial Governor's Mansion during his term.

Another noteworthy home is the Brougher-Bath house at 204 W. Spear Street. The unusual home was built in 1903-04 by Wilson Brougher, a state senator who made his fortune during Tonopah's silver strike at the turn of the century.

Brougher moved to Carson City after he purchased the Arlington Hotel on Carson Street. He built this home adjacent to the hotel — now long gone — and incorporated a number of unique design features including a two-story circular porch, stained glass windows and a wonderful circular tower that gives the structure the appearance of a castle.

The home was purchased in 1937 by Ernest Bath, the city's postmaster, who lived there with his family for more than 40 years. In recent years, it has been converted into offices but has retained its special charm.

Another interesting home is the Bender-Pozzi house at 707 W. Robinson. Built in 1866 by lawyer George Nourse, the home is associated with later owners such as David Bender, a passenger and freight agent for the Virginia & Truckee Railroad, who purchased it in 1874.

In 1901, the home was acquired by Archie Pozzi Sr., an Ormsby County commissioner, and remained in his family until 1980. The two-story house is notable for its broad curved porch that overlooks a large, manicured lawn lined with beautiful trees.

Equally impressive is the Abe Curry house at 406 N. Nevada Street. The home was built by the founder of Carson City in 1871 using native sandstone quarried from the Nevada State Prison.

Likewise, the Edwards House, located at 205 N. Minnesota, was built of native sandstone cut from the Nevada prison quarry. Visitors should also note the unusual two-story bay window in this beautiful residence that was built in 1877.

One of the most famous of Carson City's homes would have to be the Orion Clemens House at 502 N. Division. This house was owned by the older brother of famed writer Samuel Clemens, who was better known by his pen name, Mark Twain. The younger Clemens was a frequent house guest. The two-story stucco building was originally built with wood siding.

For more information or to receive a copy of the Carson City Historic Tour brochure, contact the Carson City Chamber of Commerce, 1900 S. Carson St., Carson City, NV 89701, (702) 882-1565.

The Bliss Mansion

The Grande Old Dame
of Carson City

SHE'S 120 YEARS OLD and certainly doesn't look a day over 30. In her time, she's seen Carson City grow from a town of about 3,000 to more than 38,000 people. She's had 25 governors, nearly a century of state legislators and hundreds of other elected officials walk her marble halls.

The Nevada State Capitol is without a doubt Carson City's most impressive structure. Constructed of native sandstone, the building combines elements of traditional Corinthian, Ionic and Doric architecture. The result is a building that, as the State Register noted in 1870, "any State in the union might be proud to call its own."

Despite her regal manner and bearing, one irony is that because of development around the Capitol, the building is sometimes overlooked by passersby. Older photos display a Capitol that was easily the largest in the neighborhood and a beacon for anyone entering the valley.

Yet perhaps because the building seems to be hiding in the trees, surrounded by other state structures, there is something intimate about Nevada's Capitol. It is a friendly, neighborly building. One can stand before it, inside it and around it and feel comfortable.

The building's character is also a result of the quaint, definitely 19th century touches — the octagonal cupola, the clean, white wooden trim around the roof, the elegantly arched windows and the four ornamental porticos, that resemble porches on a favorite aunt's home.

A few years ago, the state of Nevada, under the guidance of former First Lady Bonnie Bryan, published a wonderful booklet describing the history and development of the State Capitol (as well as the history of the Governor's Mansion, the state's governors and first ladies). The book quickly went out of print, but has now been reissued with a new cover and more information.

Inside, readers will find interesting historic photos and drawings showing the original plans and drawings for the building. Copy describes the often acrimonious process that occured regarding the building site, design, construction and furnishings.

The booklet also features photos and short biographies about Nevada's governors and first ladies. For instance, did you know that only seven of the 25 governors have been native Nevadans? Or that Nevada has had three foreign-born chief executives?

Additionally, the publication contains an informative history of the official Governor's Mansion, which wasn't finished until 44 years after Nevada became a state and ten governors had had to fend for themselves for accommodations.

The mansion, located at 606 Mountain in Carson City, is a beautiful example of classic colonial design. Built at an original cost of $22,700, the mansion was completed in 1909. It contains three rooms on the first floor and nine on the second floor (not including four bathrooms).

"History of the Nevada State Capitol and Governor's Mansion," is available from the Office of General Services, Capitol Complex, Carson City, NV 89710.

Nevada State Capitol

Nevada State Railroad Museum

Locomotives Found in our Own Backyard

CASEY JONES would have felt right at home in Carson City.

Over the past few years, the Nevada State Museum system has gradually developed into one of the best railroad museum facilities in the west — all in our own backyard.

Combined with Ely's fine Nevada Northern Railway Museum and the Clark County Heritage Museum in Henderson, Nevada can make a strong claim to being the railroad capital of the west.

The Nevada State Railroad Museum, located on South Carson Street at Fairview Drive, has grown from a non-descript metal building (that resembled an airplane hanger more than a museum) to a railroad theme park complete with relocated historic buildings (such as the restored Wabuska train depot), a new interpretive center, gift shop and new structures built to reflect 19th century architecture, like the new Carson City Visitor Information Center that resembles a western storefront and the unique "board and bat" square water tower.

A mile of track has been laid around the buildings so that during summer weekends (Thursday through Sunday), rides are offered on a special diesel motor car, called the *Washoe Zephyr*. On holiday weekends and special days, including the Fourth of July and Labor Day, the museum offers rides on the museum's vintage steam-powered train.

The museum also provides a wonderful opportunity to view historic Nevada railroad equipment. Over the past century, Nevada has been home to dozens of railroads ranging from national companies like Southern Pacific and Union Pacific to defunct shortlines like the Eureka & Palisades and the Virginia & Truckee (affectionately called "the V & T").

Much of the museum's collection consists of rare-vintage equipment from the famous V & T Railroad. The V & T, often called the richest shortline in the world, carried most of the silver and gold ore from Virginia City's rich mines to Reno, where it was loaded on Southern Pacific trains and taken to the rest of the world.

Inside the museum, you can see the Inyo, a wood-burning locomotive built in 1875. Polished and pretty, the Inyo is what a locomotive ought to look like. It has all the classic train design features; the shiny brass trim, massive steam smoke stack, the giant metal side-wheels, gleaming pistons and shiny black cowcatcher.

Beside it is the Dayton (the V & T was one of the few railroads that gave names to its locomotives), an equally beautiful steam snowplow engine that was built in 1882. Like its cousin, the Dayton features plenty of shiny brass and ornate wrought iron that convince you that they just don't make them like this anymore.

Other displays include several restored railroad cars, including the V & T caboose No. 9, V & T boxcar No. 1013 and the V & T flat car No. 40.

A special treat is the workshop where visitors can observe the restoration of the old railroad equipment. Here you can see the often poor condition of the equipment when it arrives at the museum and marvel at how they can make the engines and cars look so good.

Admission to the museum is $1 and there is a charge of $2.50 for adults on the steam train and $1 for the *Washoe Zephyr* motor car ride. Children are $1 for the steam train and 50-cents on the motor car.

For more information, contact the Nevada State Railroad Museum, 2180 S. Carson St., Carson City, NV 89701, (702) 885-4810 or 885-5168.

Nevada State Museum

Carson City's Private Reserve

IT'S EASY for those who live or spend a lot of time in Carson City to overlook special places or attractions that we see everyday. A case in point is the Nevada State Museum, a veritable vault of interesting historical, cultural and natural objects that is located right in the heart of the city.

The state museum is housed in the historic Carson City Mint building. Built in 1866 of native sandstone (extracted from a state prison quarry in Carson City), the mint produced some $50 million in silver and gold coins. It later served as a federal assay office, then was allowed to sit vacant for many years.

In the late 1930s, Judge Clark Guild persuaded the State Legislature to purchase the abandoned mint building for a new museum. Congress approved the sale of the building to the state in 1939 and the doors opened on Nevada Day, October 31, 1941. Since that time, the museum has increased in size and scope, adding new wings and expanding the breadth of its exhibits.

A visit to the museum is a worthwhile way to spend a few hours. After entering, the first section you encounter is a series of displays detailing the history of the mint and includes the original coin press and examples of Carson City Mint currency (unfortunately there are no free samples). Highlight of this portion is a display of an ornate silver setting made from Virginia City ore that was once used by the Navy.

The museum also contains a fine natural history section with exhibits of much of the plant and animal life indigenous to Nevada. There are excellent displays describing native birds, reptiles, fish and almost every other creature that has walked, crawled, hopped, slithered or glided across the wide Nevada landscape.

In the Indian Hall, there is a fine life-size diorama of a Paiute Indian camp that shows a typical sagebrush and grass hut, handmade baskets and tribe members performing various daily tasks such as grinding pine nuts (which were a staple in their diet).

In the same room the museum has a large collection of the beautiful handmade baskets of Dat-So-La-Lee, an early 20th century Washoe basket-weaver who became renowned for her meticulous handiwork. Some of her work has been appraised at more than $10,000.

Visitors can also view what is probably the state's most complete collection of minerals, ranging from unique opals and gems to various crystal and quartz stones.

The museum also features changing displays on subjects including wild horses in Nevada and the history of beer making in the Silver State.

Additionally, the museum has a life-style replica of a typical Nevada ghost town. The mock mining camp contains all of the standard ghost town buildings — the newspaper office, the assay office, the general store and, of course, the saloon — constructed from weathered and worn wood that looks authentic. An automated old sourdough and his mule serve as your guide in describing each building and the lifecycle of a 19th century Nevada mining camp.

From the ghost town, you can take another interesting journey into the past at the museum's replica of a 19th century mine. Along the way, you can find out what Deidesheimer square-set mine timbering means and why mining was such a dangerous profession a century ago. The mine tour also serves as the exit to the museum.

The Nevada State Museum is located at 600 North Carson Street, between Robinson and Caroline streets. For more information, contact the state museum at (702) 885-4810. Admission is $1.50 for those over 18, while those under 18 are free.

Carson River Walk

Carson's River Walk

ONE OF THE BEST things about writing this column is finding out about new places to explore from readers. Over the years, a number of columns have been a direct result of tips from people who have spent time hiking and driving in our own backyard.

Recently, I set out in search of something that one reader told me about and found something completely different but no less intriguing. The reader had mentioned that there was an abandoned Virginia & Truckee Railroad tunnel located on the banks of the Carson River near Mound House.

While I never did find the tunnel (perhaps that will be in a future book), I did reach the old V & T railroad bed and decided to follow it for a couple of hours through the rugged canyons lining the Carson River.

Despite the time of year — until about a week ago, things had been fairly mellow weatherwise in these parts — the walk turned out to be interesting, with plenty of beautiful, relatively unexploited scenery.

The railroad bed was in fairly good condition in some places, but washed out in others. While I profess to be no expert on the V & T (in fact, I mistakenly called it a narrow gauge railroad several months back — that's what I get for trusting Lucius Beebe's book on the V & T), from my research it appears that at least part of the time I followed what was once a spur from the main line to one of the many mills that once lined the river.

The hike was spectacular. Beside the railroad bed flowed the Carson River, high at this time of year and full of the power and energy that was harnessed by the mining mills. In some spots, the water was high and wide — not at all like the trickling water I normally associate with the Carson River.

Aspens and other trees line the riverbank, while the water wiggled through narrow canyons painted in different colored rock. In some places, the canyon walls were dark gray and coated with a luminous green moss, while in others they were harsh red and brown, or white and chalky.

The smell of damp sage permeated the air and, as I found out when I got home, seeped into my clothing. The constant rush of the river filled the canyon with the sounds of life, accented occasionally by chattering pairs of ducks enjoying a break from travels to warmer climates.

As I continued along the bank, I attempted to follow the ancient railroad line. At some spots it was like playing detective because the bed would disappear in a pile of rocks, then reappear ahead, just around a bend.

I found the stone foundations of bridges that once spanned wide gullies and evidence of wooden trestles that seemed to have jutted from rock walls. Here and there were rotting wooden piles of ties, scraps of rusted metal and large square nails. At some places, the railroad bed was supported by carefully-fitted stone walls, looking as solid as when it was in use.

After about two hours of walking, I reached the foundations of an old mill (the former Eureka Mill?). From appearances, the spur didn't seem to continue on much farther.

The mill foundations indicated a fairly large building constructed overlooking the river. Stone and brick walls remain standing and the grounds are littered with rusted metal shards.

From here, I retraced my steps, once again enjoying the peace, the beauty and the history.

Mound House is located about six miles east of Carson City via Highway 50. To reach the Carson River from Mound House, head about one mile south on Highland Road. There, you can park and head either east or west along the river (I traveled east).

Empire Cemetery

A Trip through the Carson River Corridor

DURING THE EARLY DAYS of Nevada's famous Comstock mining district, the Carson River was a ready source of water to operate mills that reduced the rich gold and silver ore.

Within a few years, a seven-mile portion of the Carson River between Dayton and Carson City developed into a veritable strip of mining mills. At the west end of this ribbon was the community of Empire, site of the first small mill, built in 1860. Other mills followed and eventually Empire boasted several hundred permanent residents.

Originally, ore was hauled to the mills by wagon, then later on, by the famed Virginia and Truckee Railroad, which was built in 1869 on the banks of the Carson River. The railroad made it possible to process large quantities of gold and silver ore and the Carson River mills (which carried such colorful names as The Mexican, Yellow Jacket, Brunswick, Merrimac,

Vivian and Santiago) operated successfully for more than 40 years.

Today, it is still possible to drive along the banks of the Carson River (a four-wheel drive vehicle is recommended since most of the road is not paved) and find the remnants of mills and ore piles. To reach the river, head east on Highway 50, then turn south on Deer Run Road. After about a half-mile, you will reach the river. Turn left and follow the road for as long as you want.

An historic marker about four miles east of the turnoff from Highway 395 onto Highway 50 commemorates the spot where Empire was once located. History books tell us that more than 700 people lived in Empire in the late 1860s and it contained a business district that stretched for three-quarters of a mile.

Additionally, if you turn onto an unmarked road (opposite the turn off to Centennial Park and the Eagle Valley golf courses) leading to the Nevada Western Concrete facility, you can spot an old cemetery that is the last reminder of Empire.

A short stroll through the cemetery reveals about three dozen well maintained graves, many with substantial marble headstones and wrought iron fences. From the cemetery, it is also possible to get a good view of the nearby Carson River, as it winds south of Carson City.

About a tenth-of-a-mile further east is Deer Run Road, which leads to the Carson River and the abandoned bed of the Virginia & Truckee Railroad. Even in a drought there is water in the Carson and considerable green foliage along the banks.

Driving along, one can't help but be struck by the natural beauty and with a feeling of regret that the railroad no longer winds through the river corridor. At a few places on the river I spotted campers hidden in the trees; people taking advantage of a camping area largely unknown to most.

About two miles from the point where I turned off Deer

Run Road and followed the river road, I spotted the large ruins of an abandoned mining mill. The site was located a little west of the road and appeared to have been served by its own spur from the main V & T track. Discarded rifle shells and boxes at the site also indicated that it has become popular as an informal shooting range in more recent times.

Ash Canyon

Getting Away from It All
in Ash Canyon

JUST MINUTES from downtown Carson City in the foothills of
the Sierra Nevada is a remarkable little canyon split by a picturesque bubbling stream and lined with beautiful aspens and pines.
Called Ash Canyon, it may have few peers as a haven for escap-
ing from the pressures and rigors of everyday life.

The beginning of Ash Canyon is located about two miles
north of the intersection of Ash Canyon Road and Winnie Lane.
Head north on Ash Canyon to Longview Way, then turn right
on the second dirt road. Follow the road for about a mile, heading toward a large water tower. Along the way, you will pass a
small reservoir.

The road heads up the mountain, but you can park any-
where above the water tower, then hike down into the canyon. If
you hike long enough you can reach Hobart Reservoir, which
provides some of Carson City's water.

I recently drove (then hiked) up to this special place with my son. What we found was a thin ribbon of paradise; a rushing stream cascading down a narrow canyon, tall zebra-striped aspens whose leaves have just turned brilliant gold and brown and towering green pines — certainly not what one expects in so-called high desert country.

One of the unusual things about this canyon is that it exists while surrounded by drier, desert-like terrain. The effect is to create a small oasis where you can stroll through lush alpine surroundings, listening to the rush of a mountain stream, while smelling distinctive sagebrush fragrances.

Ash Canyon is a perfect fall day hike. While there are no signs or developed trails, a path meanders beside the stream, passing a series of small waterfalls created by the canyon's slope and moss-covered rocks that have formed natural barriers.

It all makes for a great sanctuary. This is a place for peaceful contemplation amidst the trees, gentle breezes and rushing water. At several points, it's difficult not to just sit beside the stream on a carpet of tan pine needles and fallen aspen leaves and enjoy the sunlight filtering through the trees.

Toss a pinecone on the water and watch it swirl in a small pool before sliding over a natural spillway, then disappearing in a sudden rush of agitated water. Look over there and spot a tiny mushroom struggling to rise above the pine needle floor.

Naturally, there are the occasional, disruptive reminders of civilization. Just up the stream from where we started, we walked around the abandoned husk of a gray station wagon and along the way passed a half dozen empty beer bottles. Still, it's easy to forgive and overlook in such surroundings.

We hiked for about a mile and just enjoyed the sights and sounds. We passed bushes of red berries and watched grasshoppers dart across the path ahead of us. Above, a startled bird sounded our arrival, then flew on ahead to make sure everyone knew we were coming.

At one place, we found the remains of a crude aspen lean-to. Someone had chopped branches from surrounding trees and formed a rude structure. Adjacent was a round stone barbecue pit filled with recent ashes and a blackened coffee can.

All it did was remind us that below was the city and its people. Up here, the path, which can best be described as casual, continued ever upward. While we turned back after about two miles and didn't hike all the way to the source of the stream, we were sure we could have gone all the way to Lake Tahoe.

Clear Creek

Nature on Display at Clear Creek

ONE OF THE BEST — and most accessible — places to hike in this area is old Highway 50, now better known as Clear Creek Road, at the south end of Carson City.

There, literally minutes away from the city, you can drive out of the valley, park and then hike into the tall pines and clear air of the Sierra Nevada.

The road is easy to find. Just head south of Carson City on Highway 395, then take the first right after the turnoff for Lake Tahoe. The route is signed as Clear Creek Road (it runs in front of Bodine's restaurant).

Pass the Fuji Horseman's Arena and Fuji Park and head west. At about 1.3 miles, the road narrows into a scenic canyon lined by impressive cliffs. Here, rock walls, looking like the craggy, weathered faces of old men, whisper stories about the area's rich past.

If you listen real hard you can hear them tell about a time long ago when the Clear Creek Grade was the main route for getting from Carson City to Lake Tahoe. This was the Carson-Glenbrook stage route where famed driver Hank Monk whipped his horses into a froth as he raced over the mountains, his trembling passengers praying for a safe arrival.

This was also the location of the Clear Creek Canyon flume, a massive, V-shaped wooden trough that once paralleled the road and transported tens of millions of board feet of lumber from the Tahoe basin to Virginia City's mines.

Perhaps the most expressive of the ancient stone visages lining the canyon is one called the Pinnacle, a castle-like granite cluster of rock on the south side that almost seems to guard the entrance to this beautiful natural setting.

Over the past century, Clear Creek has seen the changes. Stagecoaches and mule-trains were eventually replaced by loud horseless carriages, then more quiet automobiles.

The road was finally abandoned when engineers decided that a route over nearby Spooner Summit was less steep and more inviting to travelers, and built modern Highway 50.

Since then, Clear Creek has quietly slipped into obscurity. A handful of homes in the canyon and the Clear Creek Youth Center, owned by the state of Nevada, ensure that the first four miles of the road remain in pretty good shape.

But, it is the road beyond that offers a welcome escape. As you climb higher up the grade, you notice changes in the terrain. Piñon and sage are replaced by tall pines, mountain mahogany and other mountain vegetation.

Of course, part of what makes the area special is Clear Creek, a trickling ribbon of water that rides down the canyon. Before it becomes too steep and heads up into the Sierra Nevada, the road follows the creek.

During a recent visit, the conditions were just about perfect.

The sun was high overhead, but not too hot, the creek was gurgling like a contented infant and a hint of wind would periodically rush through the trees.

Despite the fact I was hiking along a paved road, there was still a feeling of solitude, of being somewhere where people hadn't been for a long time. Perhaps it was because the road was cracked and broken in many places — downright impassable for a vehicle — as if nature was trying to shed the asphalt armor and expose her long-covered skin to the sun once more.

Or it was because the higher you climbed the better you could hear the wind and the birds and the stream? And while high above and to the north was Highway 50, you would hardly know it was there.

The road continues over the mountains — a full day's hike — and ends up near the intersection of Highways 50 and 28 near Glenbrook.

King's Canyon

History and Scenic Splendor
in King's Canyon

PREVIOUSLY, I wrote about Clear Creek Grade, once one of the major routes leading from Carson City to Lake Tahoe. An equally beautiful and historic road is located in King's Canyon, directly west of Carson City.

Here, visitors will find another of the original trails that a century ago aided in the development of both Carson City and Virginia City.

According to the late E. B. Scott's wonderful *Saga of Lake Tahoe* books, King's Canyon was first known as Lake Bigler Toll Road (Bigler being an earlier name for Lake Tahoe). The road was built in 1863 by engineer Butler Ives and was financed by a consortium that needed another route for bringing timber to Virginia City via Carson City.

As with Clear Creek, King's Canyon was the site of an extensive system of flumes and log chutes. While nothing of the flume remains, the road is a pleasant hiking, mountain-biking or four-wheeling trip for local residents.

An interesting historic note is that in 1870, mining magnates William Sharon and William Ralston decided to determine whether Clear Creek or King's Canyon was the faster route. Ralston challenged Sharon to a race from Carson to Glenbrook at Lake Tahoe.

History tells us that Sharon drove his horse so hard that it went blind and he forfeited the contest to Ralston.

Today, travelers can find the historic road by heading west on King Street. The paved road ends about four miles from downtown Carson City. From here, the road isn't paved, but is in fairly good condition.

About a quarter-mile from the end of the paved road you can overlook a picturesque meadow. Behind is a splendid view of Carson City; the state Capitol looking like some kind of silver-domed doll house.

Around the road are small clusters of pine amidst the sage-brush. About a half-mile up you come to a pastoral setting — fine green pasture land bordered by poplar tree towers and a barbed wire fence.

During my recent hike, I could hear, but not see, sheep bleating in the vicinity. Down below the road there was a small round trailer, presumably the temporary home of a shepherd.

Standing there among the trees, under the deep blue sky, I was reminded of writer Robert Laxalt's introduction in his book *Sweet Promised Land*: "My father was a sheepherder, and his home was the hills."

While I never saw the sheepman, I recalled Laxalt's description of the type of men who did this work, and imagined what he must be like — "These were the men of leather and bronze who had been rich as barons one day and broke and working for wages the next, who had ridden big and powerful horses, and who had met in the lonely desert and talked a while, hunkering over a sagebrush fire and a blackened coffeepot, and even though they had battled with life, they had learned to accept it, because they had learned first to bow their heads to the winter blizzards and the desert sun."

And I knew he would earn his wages. Ahead, for just a moment, I spotted a coyote warily crossing the road, then disappearing into the trees.

This is the real Nevada where the desert and mountains join and the china-blue sky and green-grey earth meet. Here is a place where one can learn the true meaning of the word, awesome (long before it was discovered by teenage mutant ninja turtles and valley girls), and understand how mighty is the power of the creator.

The road continues for more than 11 miles to the summit. Along the way, you pass the original location of several historic ranches, including the Heidenreich and John Quill spreads.

There are also a series of beautiful, green "canyon-ettes" along the road that feature small waterfalls and a wide variety of lush vegetation, including ferns, berries and other foliage. About nine miles from Carson City is the former site of Swift's Station, once a stagecoach stop.

PART II

Comstock Country

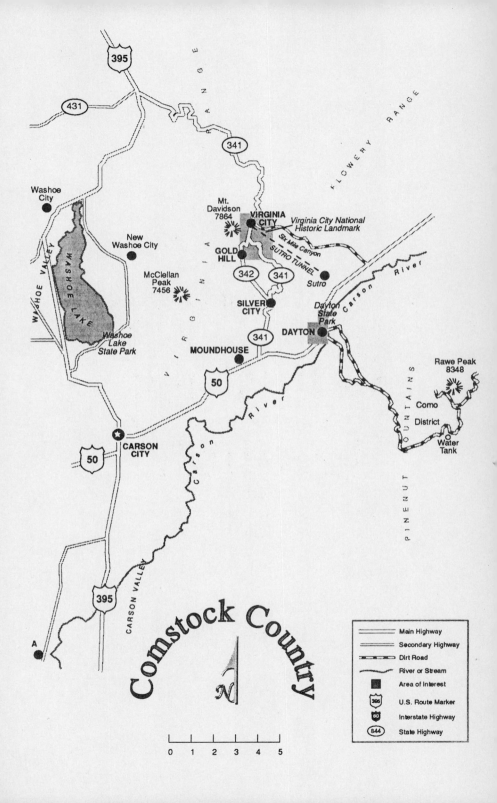

Comstock Country

IF THE MAGNIFICENT Comstock Lode had never been discovered, the state of Nevada would not exist.

In the late 1840s and early 1850s, Nevada was little more than miles of empty land containing a couple of trading posts and a few farming plots cultivated by Mormon missionaries sent out from Salt Lake City by Brigham Young.

The region's main reason for being seemed to be to bedevil settlers and gold miners heading west to the promised land of California.

But the discovery of some bluish mud and a few gold specks forever changed Nevada's image. By the late 1850s, gold and huge quantities of silver had been discovered in the shadow of Sun Mountain, just east of the Sierra Nevada.

The discovery site, which became known as the Comstock Lode, created wealth and attracted thousands of people to Nevada. Communities sprouted almost overnight with names like Gold Hill, Silver City, Dayton and the majestic Queen of the Comstock, Virginia City.

The Comstock Country is Nevada's oldest and most historic region. But, as oldtimers will tell you, it is more than simply a place. It is a way of life, a state of mind, a philosophy and an attitude that helps explain the development of the Nevada character and personality.

It is charming drunks like James Fenimore, a proud native Virginian who "christened" and named Virginia City after he dropped a whiskey bottle on a hard packed dirt street of a then-unnamed mining camp. It is enterprising con men like Henry Comstock, who actually discovered nothing other than a way to take credit for the fabulous silver and gold strike that bears his name.

It is dreamers like Adolph Sutro, who believed, when no others did, that he would build a massive tunnel to drain hot water from the Comstock Lode's mines. It is writers, like young Sam Clemens, who honed his skills chronicling the colorful characters and incredible stories of the area, and forever captured the soul of the American frontier.

Comstock Country is a place where you can still find the remains of the head frames, train tracks and classic western-style storefronts that defined the era.

The following stories are an invitation to wander along the aging boardwalks, past the faded wooden and brick buildings of the region that was once called the richest place on earth.

Discover Washoe Valley's Historic Sites

ONE OF THE BEST reasons to drive from Carson City to Reno is being able to pass through beautiful Washoe Valley.

The eight-mile stretch from the top of Lakeview (the hill at the north end of Carson City) to the rise at the northern end of Little Washoe Lake is a special treat for travelers. The snow-capped mountains (which, by the way, is what Sierra Nevada means) that line the western side of Washoe Valley are among the most scenic in northwestern Nevada.

While the most efficient way to cross through Washoe Valley is Highway 395, a leisurely and enjoyable way to travel is to depart from 395 at East Lake Boulevard (called exit 42), then follow Old Highway 395.

Life immediately becomes less harried on the old highway, which now serves as a parallel frontage road. Rather than racing through Washoe Valley on the 395 raceway, this road begs for casual travel.

There are actually two faces to Washoe Valley. On the eastern side, the terrain is rather dry, resembling the kind of high desert that describes most of Nevada. But on the west side — the side where the old highway runs — the environment is more lush and green, akin to Lake Tahoe or the Carson Valley.

Driving along, you can see the kind of rural Nevada that is rapidly disappearing in the northwestern part of the state. Over there is a flock of sheep grazing in a grassy field. Up the road is a sprawling ranch with acres of fertile grassland and a half-dozen horses huddled under a shade tree.

At about the three-mile point, you reach Franktown Road, a worthwhile sidetrip. Turn left and notice how the surroundings change even more. Instead of the openness of the valley, you begin to drive through clusters of tall pine trees. The air is even cooler.

Ranches here seem to take on more ostentatious names; the "Lightning W," "Windy J," and the "Washoe Pines," are just a few. The livestock even becomes a bit more exotic, with ranches boasting Arabians and other show horses.

Additionally, the homes become more impressive. Hidden among the tall trees are massive Tudor and Edwardian-style castles, sprawling country estates and even one more contemporary glass and wood monolith featuring a veritable wall of windows overlooking the valley (I'd certainly hate to be responsible for cleaning them) and a large statue of a Chinese lion.

The Franktown area was one of the first to be settled in Nevada. In the early 1850s, Mormon pioneers established farms in the foothills. Within three years, a small community was laid out, which included one of the region's first sawmills.

In the late 1850s, most of the Mormon settlers were called to return to Utah during a dispute between the church and the U.S. Government. Their lands were acquired — often illegally — by the remaining residents.

About that time, a large stamp mill was built in Franktown to process the gold and silver ore that had been discovered in nearby Virginia City. However, by the mid-1860s, the mine owners decided to shift ore-processing operations closer to the mines and the facility was dismantled.

Within a few years, most of the commercial development associated with Franktown disappeared, and the area assumed the pastoral agricultural identity that it retains today.

Franktown Road rejoins the old highway after a five-mile loop. A state historical marker located near the intersection provides a brief but interesting history of Franktown. Behind the marker is an abandoned farmhouse that looks like it may be one of the last remnants of the old town.

About a mile from the Franktown intersection is Bowers Mansion. This impressive two-story building was built in 1864 by Lemuel S. "Sandy" Bowers and his wife, Eilley Orrum Bowers, who are among the first millionaires created by the fabulous mining wealth in Virginia City.

As if to compensate for their humble beginnings — Sandy Bowers was an illiterate Scottish prospector and his wife a former boardinghouse keeper — the Bowers' furnished the mansion with fine European furniture and trappings collected during several trips abroad.

Sandy died a few years after the house was built and Eilley continued to live there, even after the money ran out. Ultimately, she was forced to sell the brick mansion and returned to Virginia City, where she lived out her days telling fortunes. The mansion was eventually sold to Washoe County, which restored it to its previous splendor.

Surrounding the mansion is one of the most complete recreational complexes in the area, operated by the Washoe County Parks Department. In addition to tours of the mansion during the summer months, visitors can enjoy a geothermal-heated

47

swimming pool, picnic grounds, horseshoe pits and several sand volleyball courts. There are three group picnic areas which can be reserved.

A mile from Bowers Mansion, the landscape becomes barren and rocky — as if the ground had been ripped up by some giant's rage. The truth is that several years ago, a massive rock slide washed down the mountain and across the road here depositing tons of mud and rocks. In fact, it is because the area is prone to slides that the large mountain overlooking this part of Washoe Valley is called Slide Mountain.

A little farther up the road is another historical marker detailing the history of another community that was formerly in Washoe Valley. Called Ophir, all that remains are stone walls located adjacent to Highway 395 and Washoe Lake.

A half-mile from the marker is Davis Creek Park, a quiet, shaded campground and hiking area also operated by Washoe County. Here you will find camping sites, marked hiking trails, a nature walk and group picnic areas.

For more information about Bowers Mansion Park, call 849-1825. For group picnic reservations at either Bowers or Davis Creek, call 785-4319. For Davis Creek camping information call 849-0684.

Washoe Valley

Memories of the V & T
in Washoe Valley

OPERATING FROM 1869 to 1950, the Virginia & Truckee Railroad was an integral part of Nevada's mining history and an important transportation link in Northern Nevada.

While the best place to see the V & T's historic locomotives and cars is at the Nevada State Railroad Museum in Carson City, it is possible to find other remnants of the famed rail line, which ran from Reno to Virginia City, if you retrace the train's route.

One particularly interesting short hike is to view the remains of two train trestles located at the north end of Washoe Valley. Maps of the V & T route indicate that rather than passing over the hill, the train traveled through a narrow canyon stretching from Pleasant Valley to Washoe Valley.

The two V & T train trestles at the north end of Washoe Valley are located about 12 miles north of Carson City via Highway 395.

Park near the Amsterdam Antiques, then hike into the adjacent canyon.

At the entrance to the canyon was the community of Washoe City. In the early 1860s, Washoe City became the county seat and grew to a population of about 6,000 people.

Today, the only remains of the town are the walls of one of the old commercial buildings and the cemetery, located near the Cattlemen's restaurant. Additionally, near the entrance to the canyon you can find the foundations for some kind of structure and a fine example of a hand-dug well.

About a quarter-mile from Highway 395, as you head into the canyon, you will find the first trestle. The thick vertical wooden beams still span a small creek and rest upon a sandstone and slate foundation. No rails or ties remain on the trestle, but you can see the railroad bed stretching north into the canyon.

The canyon itself is intriguing. The walls are pocked and rough like the skin of an ancient cowboy. Walking through the narrow passage, the only sound is the wind which seems at times to mimic the sound of a V & T train whistle.

Another 500 yards or so is the second trestle. This bridge is more complete than the other, boasting a handful of vertical beams and horizontal ties. Along the banks of the creek (it's the same small stream, which snakes through the canyon) you can see the intricate stonework of the foundations.

The bed continues on through the canyon but quickly becomes impassable. I counted the supports for at least two other bridges that once existed further up the line.

Scattered about the canyon are a few loose rail ties. After the train was discontinued in 1950, the rails were ripped up and sold. In most places, the rail bed is difficult to follow through forty years of unchecked sagebrush, shrubs and grass.

Yet despite the neglect and ravages of time, there is something precious about seeing the trestles and reliving — if only in your mind — the glory days of the railroad that was once one of the richest in the world.

V&T remnants

Gardnerville

A Sunday Drive through the Carson Valley

WHEN MY SISTER and I were kids, my parents used to pile us into the family car for a Sunday drive.

We were never sure where my father, who would always do the driving, planned to take us — and I'm not certain he always knew — but we looked forward to those journeys into the unknown.

For those of us fortunate to live in this area, there are plenty of wonderful places to take that proverbial Sunday drive, including south to the Carson Valley.

Located about a dozen miles south on U.S. Highway 395, the Carson Valley is a fertile region that includes the twin cities of Minden and Gardnerville.

Minden is a quiet farming town that has, in recent years become a popular residential community. The community was established in 1905 when the Virginia and Truckee Railroad extended a line south of Carson City to transport agricultural products from the Carson Valley.

Today, the town has a very distinctive charm. Local builders have attempted to maintain a certain architectural integrity, constructing turreted buildings that incorporate natural materials, like brick, wood and stone into a pleasing modified Tudor design.

The Carson Valley Inn, one of the premier examples of the town's "look," is also one of those friendly inns and casinos that you find in the more rural parts of the state. The inn offers reasonably priced rooms and several restaurants serving great food.

The community park in Minden has a tidy, Norman Rockwell-esque quality with its round bandstand and manicured grass. The biggest event each year is the Carson Valley Days in mid-June, during which the park overflows with people enjoying the early summer weather, fine arts and crafts, a variety of games and a marvelous Basque barbecue.

The Nevada Basque culture is well represented in nearby Gardnerville, just south of Minden. Perhaps no other place in the state, save Elko and Winnemucca, can offer as many quality Basque restaurants as you can find in Gardnerville.

Hungry travelers can enjoy Basque family-style meals at the J&T Bar and the Overland Hotel on Main Street in the center of the town, or continue to the south end of the city to the Carson Valley Country Club.

Each serves sumptuous meals of beef, lamb and fish, depending on availability, along with massive quantities of wholesome soups, salad, french fries and side dishes that can include anything from Basque beans to sauteed beef tongue. Since Basque meals are served family-style, they just keep serving you until you're full.

Another legendary Carson Valley chow house is Sharkey's. For more than two decades, Sharkey's has been serving the largest slab of prime rib in the universe (okay, I might be exaggerating a little, but it sure seems that way). The menu also includes giant hamburgers, thick steaks and other tasty items.

While at Sharkey's, make sure to wander the casino and study the walls. Nearly every open space is filled with an eclectic mixture of historical signs, political campaign posters, boxing paraphernalia, vintage license plates, circus posters and other interesting things.

In fact, the walk to the restrooms is a journey down memory lane for boxing fans. The walls are covered with old boxing photos, many autographed, of famous pugilists. The bar also contains a large collection of saddles, spurs, ropes and other beautiful cowboy artifacts.

For more information, contact the Carson Valley Chamber of Commerce, Box 1200, Minden, NV 89423, (702) 782-8144.

Genoa

Genoa: First in the Heart of Nevada

NESTLED IN THE SHADOWS of the eastern Sierra Nevada range, Genoa has long been a special place in Nevada.

In 1851, Mormon traders settled in the area — making it the first permanent settlement in what would become the state of Nevada — to provide provisions for the wagon trains that had just completed the difficult journey across Nevada and Utah.

Called the Mormon Station, the post quickly developed into a small but important farming community. However, in 1857, Brigham Young recalled Mormons throughout the west to Salt Lake City because of a dispute with the federal government.

Many of the Mormons abandoned their homes and farms or settled for token payments. This ultimately let to disagreements and in 1862, Orson Hyde, a Mormon elder who found his land confiscated by non-Mormons in his absence actually placed a curse on the area residents in the hope of frightening them into paying for the property.

The town survived the curse and a name change in the early 1860s to Genoa (which is pronounced Guh-no-uh, not Jen-no-a, as it is in Italy).

For a time, the growing town became the center of activity in the region. From 1860-61, it was a stop on the famous Pony Express route and a rest station for travelers on the Overland Stageline. In 1864, Genoa became the seat of Douglas County in the new state of Nevada.

Around that time, Genoa also became home for several of the state's earliest newspapers, including the Territorial Enterprise, which would later relocate to Virginia City where it became one of the west's most beloved and famous periodicals. Among those who worked on the Territorial Enterprise was Mark Twain.

Being first doesn't always guarantee success. Within a few years, Genoa was eclipsed in importance by other communities in northwestern Nevada, such as booming Virginia City and Reno. By the 1880s, Genoa could only claim a few hundred people and a handful of businesses.

Indeed, several fires over the years succeeded in decimating much of the original town. One story is that the worst fire in 1910 was started by a resident of the county poor farm who lit a pan of sulfur beneath his bed to rid himself of the bedbugs. The mattress caught on fire and sparked a fire that destroyed half the business district and the original Mormon Fort (which, to be quite frank, had never reached landmark status, having been used over the years as a chicken coop and a pig barn).

In 1916, Genoa was replaced as the county seat by Minden, a newer ranching and farming community located closer to the major highways. Despite the loss, the town never joined the ranks of Nevada's ghost towns.

Perhaps because of its magnificent picturesque setting in the Sierra pines, Genoa has survived. The splendid, two-story brick courthouse, built in 1865, was used as a school from 1916 to

1956, then was converted into a fine, small museum. The site of the Mormon Fort became the location of a shaded state park that features a replica of the old fort, which also houses a museum.

Additionally, one of Genoa's true claims to immortality is that it is home of the famous Genoa Bar — the oldest saloon in the state. From its uneven floor to its worn wood and brass counter to the ancient chandeliers hanging from the ceiling, the Genoa Bar is a genuine Nevada landmark and worthy of a visit if only for a tall, cool one.

The town is filled with quaint, friendly buildings and homes that echo the region's past. If you walk the unpaved side streets you can find plenty of half-hidden gems, such as the lovely Genoa House, originally constructed in the 1860s, which is now a bed and breakfast located in the town's oldest neighborhood.

In recent years, Genoa has become increasingly popular as a residential area by people willing to invest a little time and effort into restoring the graceful Victorian homes perched overlooking the nearby Carson Valley.

Befitting its reputation as an open, friendly town, Genoa's most important annual special event is the Candy Dance, traditionally held in late September. The event, which attracts hundreds each year, features a large craft fair and a candy festival with dozens of homemade candies, fudge, cookies and other delectables. Highlighted is an old-fashioned, down-home community dance — the Candy Dance.

Just minutes from Genoa is Walley's Hot Springs, a geothermal resort offering relaxing, natural hot pools, accommodations and a first class restaurant.

For more information about Genoa, contact the Carson Valley Chamber of Commerce, (702) 782-8144.

Odeon Hall, Dayton

Rediscover the Comstock
in Dayton

HISTORY SAYS that Dayton was the site of Nevada's first marriage — and divorce.

According to the records — which are detailed in David Toll's excellent book, *The Compleat Nevada Traveler* — a prospector searching for a silver strike returned to the then-new hamlet of Dayton to find his 14-year-old daughter had married in his absence.

The miner grabbed his offspring and fled for California, with the indignant bridegroom and townspeople in hot pursuit. The two parties met on the road and decided to let the girl choose her future.

Perhaps predicting a future Nevada industry, the young woman opted for a quick Nevada divorce, then headed off with her father to the sunshine of the Golden State where, presumably, she lived happily ever after.

Dayton, located 12 miles east of Carson City on Highway 50, remains one of the most interesting pockets of Nevada history. The community was originally a trading post and, after the discovery of silver in Virginia City, became one of the Comstock's first mill sites.

In the late 1850s, Chinese workers were brought into the area to construct a ditch from the Carson River to the entrance of Gold Canyon. The workers established a small settlement, thereby providing the town with its first name, "Chinatown." In 1861, a town was formally laid out and named for the surveyor, John Day.

Today, Dayton is a quiet but growing community. The heart of the town is its historic downtown, which contains many 19th century buildings, including the Odeon Hall, a dance hall and saloon built in the 1870s. The Odeon, which house's Mia's Swiss Restaurant, once hosted ex-President Ulysses S. Grant.

Dayton is a great place to just wander and explore. The town has a number of historic markers that provide interesting information about the many old stone buildings and sites.

The greatest congregation of markers (seemingly in the state) is along Highway 50, near the turn to the downtown. There, no less than three detail the stories behind the town's former name of Chinatown, the community's rich history as the second oldest town in Nevada and its role as part of the Pony Express route in the 1860s.

Just outside of the downtown area, at Main Street and Cemetery Road, is another marker commemorating the former location of Hall's Station, site of the state's first New Year's Eve dance in 1853. And across the street, is the beautifully-restored Bluestone Building, which is now county offices and a court.

Dayton was also the home of the corrals for Nevada's legendary camel corps. A marker tells the story of the attempt in the 1860s to use camels to haul wood and salt to the nearby

Virginia City mines. Unfortunately, the camels spooked any horses and were eventually banned from traveling on the main roads, thereby diminishing their value as beasts of burden.

Surprisingly for a town its size, Dayton houses a number of quality restaurants, including Mia's, the End of the Trail and Misfit's. The latter is named for the fact that part of the famous movie, *The Misfits*, which featured Clark Gable, Montgomery Clift and Marilyn Monroe, was filmed in Dayton.

A good time to visit the town is on the weekends, when the Dayton Flea Market is operating. On a recent visit, sellers were peddling fresh plums and peaches, tools and a variety of other interesting wares.

For more information contact the Dayton Chamber of Commerce, Box 408, Dayton, NV 89403, (702) 246-0525.

Como ruins

Carson City's
Ghostly Neighbor

WHEN WE THINK about Nevada ghost towns, we automatically think about places located in the more remote places in the state. Yet, about 20 miles from the heart of Carson City are the remains of a mining ghost town called Como.

Como is located 10 miles southeast of Dayton in the Pine Nut Mountains. To reach it, head east of Highway 50 on Dayton Valley Road.

Turn south on a dirt road that branches off from the paved road leading to Dayton High School. Ahead, you will see the community water tank. Continue driving on the main dirt road (do not take any of the smaller branch roads) for about eight miles and you will reach Como and the former Como mining district.

Como actually grew out of another town, which no longer exists, named Palmyra. Gold was discovered in the area in 1860 and the earlier town came into being. Within two years, several hundred miners toiled in Palmyra's mines.

However, mining activity soon shifted to a site about a half-mile east of Palmyra. This new community, called Como, began to boom, and within a few years claimed a steam-driven mill, a hotel, bars, meeting hall and a weekly newspaper.

Como's mines did not contain a great amount of ore and the mines began to close in the mid-1860s. The camp was able to briefly revive in 1879 and just after the turn of the century. A large mill was built in the 1930s — but was never used since promoters discovered there was no ore left in the area.

The drive to Como from Dayton is short but interesting. After passing the Dayton High School you begin heading south into the Pine Nut mountains. The day I made the drive, I passed about eight wild horses grazing to the west.

The dirt road, while rough in places, is fairly well maintained because it is the access road to the Christmas tree cutting area at Como Pass. During December, the National Forest Service issues permits to allow the cutting of piñon pines for Christmas trees.

About five miles from the turn-off, the road becomes more steep. If you stop to look back, you can get an outstanding view of the Dayton Valley, which in the fall is filled with beautiful fall colors.

You finally reach the earliest mining remains at about the eight-mile point. The first thing you notice is a large wheel perched atop the remains of a concrete and wooden structure. The remains create wonderful shapes, with storage tanks, pylons, beams and rusted pipes.

Here, you can also find two lovely ponds fed from a spring coming out of the remains of a collapsed mine. These pools are surrounded by high grass and cat tails; one is shaded by two large trees that have turned a beautiful shade of yellow.

Around the site are the foundations of other buildings. Over there, a rusted iron broiler sits on the ground adjacent to the skeletal ruins of a tin and wooden two-story shed. Up on the hill is the rusted cylinder of a giant water tank.

Elusive mountain bluebirds flit from piñon to sagebrush. All about are the mounds of mining tails; piles of dirt bleached tan and white and devoid of all minerals and nutrients.

When the wind whistles through the groves of piñons on the hillsides and the sun ducks behind a cloud, the effect is one of eerie stillness, of truly standing in a ghost town, and of understanding the harsh and lonely life of a prospector in 19th century Nevada.

Hiking around the remains yielded a few surprises. Above the camp is the mouth of a mining tunnel. I peeked inside to see two tunnel branches, one heading east to a dead end, while the other gradually slopes down to the north and out of sight.

I touched the tunnel walls, noting that the rock was soft and crumbled with a bit of pressure. It is with good reason that officials are always urging hikers and explorers not to enter an abandoned mining tunnel.

Further up the road are the remains of the townsite of Como. Today, not much remains except for a few foundations and cellars.

Sutro Tunnel

Tunnel is Engineering
Marvel

ADOLPH SUTRO had a big dream. He dreamed that if someone drilled a long, horizontal shaft below Virginia City's fabulous mines it could drain all the natural hot water that often threatened the lives of those working in the mine shafts.

He also figured that someone could make a lot of money by building this great tunnel to drain the mines.

He also dreamed of establishing a new town southeast of Virginia City that would overtake that city in importance. Naturally, this new, planned community would be called "Sutro."

Today, you can find the remains of Sutro's dream about one mile north of U.S. Highway 50, at a point about two miles northeast of Dayton. An historical marker on the highway indicates the location of Sutro's Tunnel.

Sutro was a Prussian immigrant who arrived in Virginia City in 1860. Only 30 years old, he previously operated a successful merchandising business in San Francisco and had earlier attempted to start a store in California's gold country.

In the early 1860s, Sutro pitched his tunnel to the powers-that-be, but was generally ignored as a dreamer. In 1865, however, he persuaded the Nevada State Legislature to grant him permission to drill a four-mile long tunnel into Mount Davidson. He noted that the tunnel would provide better ventilation and would be an easier way to extract ore from Virginia City's mines.

Within a year, Sutro persuaded nearly two dozen of the Comstock Lode's largest mines to pay for each ton of ore transported through the tunnel.

Due to opposition from Virginia City bankers — who feared his dream tunnel would allow him to wrestle control of the Comstock — it took him another three years before he could arrange financing, and on October 19, 1869, work began on Sutro's hole.

Nearly nine years later, on July 8, 1878, the tunnel was completed. It cost $3.5 million and stretched more than 20,000 feet from the mouth, located just east of Dayton, to the first connection at the Savage Mine.

Unfortunately for its investors, the tunnel was completed about a decade after the mines had begun a gradual decline so that while it served its purpose, it was never the money-maker that Sutro envisioned. As a result, the tunnel never paid for itself.

As if he sensed this, Sutro quietly unloaded his stock in the venture — making more than a million dollars in profit — shortly after the tunnel was completed. He successfully invested his funds in real estate in San Francisco, eventually becoming mayor of that city.

As for Sutro's town, he succeeded in getting it started in 1870. Sutro claimed that his town would eventually surpass Virginia City and, by 1876, it would have nearly 800 residents, a school, a hospital, a church, a newspaper and Sutro's impressive Victorian mansion.

Once the tunnel was completed, the town began to decline. The final blow was a fire in 1941 that destroyed Sutro's magnificent mansion. Today, there is little more than the tunnel, a few modest houses and mountains of tunnel tailings to mark the location of the community.

Viewing Sutro's tunnel, you get a feeling you're seeing something very old and very special. In its day, the tunnel was an engineering marvel equal to an Empire State Building or a Hoover Dam.

Staring into the tunnel's blackness, you can imagine the dangers faced by tunnel workers. A thin gutter still carries water from the far-off mine shafts of Virginia City to a tepid pond near the entrance.

Despite being completed too late to have much impact on the Comstock era, the tunnel was used for drainage for more than 50 years and served a useful purpose. Indeed, the tunnel was partially restored in the 1970s by a mining company that thought it might still be useful.

But Sutro's dream that the tunnel would be a conduit for millions of tons of ore — and transform the desert around the tunnel's entrance into a great metropolis — never became a reality.

C Street, Virginia City

Wandering in Virginia City

IT'S QUIET in Virginia City in the winter. Snow has dusted Mt. Davidson — which many old timers insist should be called by its traditional name, Sun Mountain — and the summer crowds are long gone.

That also means it's the best time to wander the streets of the self-proclaimed Queen of the Comstock and reflect on her importance to the development of Nevada and the American West.

Virginia City is located 15 miles southeast of Reno via U.S. Highway 395 and Nevada State Route 341.

It was in 1859 that two miners, Peter Riley and Pat McLaughlin, found a rich gold vein in the Six Mile Canyon, an area between what is now Virginia City and Dayton. The gold was found caked in an odd blue-black dirt, which became a troublesome blue mud when mixed with water, which was necessary when placer mining for gold.

During the next few months, many a miner would curse the "blasted blue stuff" that embraced the precious gold nuggets and flakes like an unwanted hug from an overbearing aunt. It was a tedious process to extract the gold from the mud, which was either washed away into the Carson River or piled in heaps around the mining camp.

Eventually, someone finally had the good sense to find if there was any value in the blue dirt. Incredibly, the stuff turned out to be the richest silver ore ever found — and the Comstock mining boom was on.

Over the years, the mines of Virginia City produced more than a billion dollars in gold and silver and created more millionaires than television evangelism.

From its humble roots, Virginia City grew to be one of the most cosmopolitan cities in the west. Within a few years, it boasted an opera house, fine hotels and restaurants and majestic churches.

Despite a disastrous fire in 1875, Virginia City has survived into the 20th century with most of its 19th century charm and appearance. Today, it continues to offer some of the best examples of western frontier architecture.

There remains something special about walking Virginia City's uneven wooden sidewalks under aged, drooping awnings. The false store fronts and Victorian-style homes built on the steep hillside don't appear to have changed much since the days when a young Samuel Clemens was writing for the local newspaper under his pen name, "Mark Twain."

Several of the mansions of Virginia City's mining magnates remain standing and a few are open for visits. For instance, you can tour the red brick Mackay Mansion, originally the headquarters of the Gould & Curry Mine, then the residence of John Mackay, one of Virginia City's fabulously wealthy silver kings.

The nearby Chollar Mansion, built in the 1870s, has recently become a bed and breakfast, offering an opportunity to spend a night in a room built for a millionaire.

The Castle on B Street, open during the summer months, was built in 1863 by Robert Greaves, superintendent of the Empire Mine. The home was constructed by builders imported from Europe, then filled with furnishings from around the world. Inside, you can still view much of its original furniture and a remarkable three-story tower that offers a panoramic view of the entire city.

The Presbyterian Church on C Street, built in 1867, was one of the few structures on that block that didn't succumb to flames during the fire of 1875. Down the hill is the magnificent St. Mary's in the Mountains Catholic Church and the St. Paul's Episcopalian Church, both rebuilt to their previous splendor in the years immediately after the fire.

No visit to Virginia City should overlook Piper's Opera House, located on B Street. Built in 1885, the present wooden building is actually the third opera house built on that site (the others burned).

Inside, the opera house, which still offers live performances, hasn't changed much from the days when touring acting and singing companies would stop by to perform Shakespeare for the miners.

Virginia City's C Street is lined with small shops offering souvenirs, antiques, homemade candies, tee shirts, restaurants, small museums and plenty of saloons.

Not surprisingly, the saloons are where some of Virginia City's history can often best be found. Nearly every bar boasts some kind of historical shrine, ranging from the Silver Queen's wall-size painting of a woman wearing a dress consisting of dozens of priceless silver dollars and gold coins to the Delta Saloon's "Suicide Table," a card table that brought bad luck to many of its previous owners.

One unique item available at the Union Brewery Saloon is locally-brewed beer. A recent change in state law allowed the Union Brewery to be the only "brew-pub" (meaning it can brew its own beer) in the state. The saloon also has an extensive beer memorabilia collection.

The museums, which all charge nominal admission fees, include: the new Nevada Gambling Museum, which has a fine collection of vintage slot machines and gaming devices; the Nevada State Fire Museum & Comstock Firemen's Museum, which is jammed with rare fire equipment that was used to fight the devastating blazes the seemed to threaten the town every few years; a Mark Twain museum; and the "Way It Was Museum," featuring a large collection of antique mining equipment.

To the south of town is the impressive Fourth Ward School, which is now a museum. Built in 1876, the restored four-story structure once housed nearly 1,000 students and was the most modern school of its day (it had indoor plumbing on all four floors).

However, in the end, the real fun about Virginia City isn't only the fudge shops, the museums and the bars. It is the feel of being in a place which has somehow resisted most change and retained its unique, shopworn frontier character.

For more information, contact the Virginia City Chamber of Commerce, V & T Railroad Car, C Street, Virginia City, NV 89440, (702) 847-0311.

Nevada's Funky Brewery

I GLANCE OVER to an ancient wooden door at the rear of the saloon and notice the doorknob is jiggling — like someone is trying to turn it — but I see no one through the door's glass window. I figure it must either be a very short person or a poltergeist.

I start toward the door to let either one in and bartender Julie Hoover stops me.

"Don't worry about it, it's only Jasper," she says.

The door opens and a gray and black cat strolls into the room. Right then I know there must be something really special about this tasty dark, foamy beer I've been sipping.

~

Rick and Julie Hoover operate the first brewery opened in

Nevada in more than 30 years (since the Reno Brewing Company closed in 1956). Their Union Brewery in Virginia City is the first "micro-brewery" in Nevada and the state's only beer house.

The Hoovers began serving their unique brand of beer in October of 1987 following a change in the state law that allows them to brew up to 500 barrels of draft a year (about 16,000 gallons). The beer is special — the only place you can purchase and drink it is on the premises of the Union Brewery, a combination brewery and saloon.

Until recently, state law restricted breweries to the Comstock Historic District (basically Virginia City, Gold Hill and Silver City). As a result, for the past four years, the Hoovers had the market all to themselves when it came to Nevada-produced beer.

Interestingly, the Hoovers are riding the crest of a wave of "boutique" breweries in the country. In the past decade, many states, including California and Oregon, have relaxed their laws to allow beer to be sold on the same premises it is made.

At the same time, the public is showing indications it is willing to accept beers that are a little heavier or full-bodied than the lighter lagers sold by most national beer companies. Proof of that is the virtual explosion in home-brewing during the past few years.

"If you have a glass of this and then drink Budweiser or Miller, you'll think they taste like water," notes Rick Hoover.

Hoover, along with brewer John Buie, developed the formula for the Union Brewery's brew. They brew about 45 gallons every five days. The process for making the beer is fairly simple; after the liquid is brewed, it is aged about five weeks in a refrigerated chamber. From that room, it is piped at a cool 36 degrees directly to a tap upstairs. Beer doesn't come any fresher.

The basement of the C Street saloon has been converted into a small glass-enclosed production line with a row of stainless steel vats and tanks. The opposite side of the room is lined with more than 500 rare and unique beer cans and bottles.

Hoover has converted part of the basement into a brewery museum. In addition to the display case, which includes famous Nevada beer names such as Sierra Beer, Tahoe Beer and my favorite, One Sound State Beer, the museum features beer trays, antique brewing equipment and other saloon paraphernalia.

Brewer Buie often holds court in the basement, pouring glasses of the saloon's special brew, giving tours of the facility and the museum and generally talking about beer.

Hoover says the new beer has helped business, particularly during the slower winter months. The Hoovers, who have lived in Virginia City for about a decade, have operated the Union Brewery saloon on the first floor for the past four years.

Part of the charm of drinking a glass of Union Brewery Beer is the ambience. The saloon is one of those old brick Virginia City bars that literally oozes with character.

In one corner is an Australian flag, while another wall is lined with yellowed boxing posters and photographs. A dried Christmas tree covered with brassieres hangs upside down from the ceiling — it is a source of much conversation — while faded VFW banners are draped over other walls. I even spotted a re-elect Rex Bell for Lieutenant Governor poster. Bell was a former B-movie western actor who died in 1962.

As with most Virginia City buildings, the brewery has a long history. According to the Nevada Historical Society, the Union Saloon opened in 1862. Two years later, it moved to a new location under a new owner under the name Union Brewery Saloon.

The building burned down in 1865, but was rebuilt (although Hoover says the side walls are the originals, dating back to 1864). It continued to be used as a brewery under various owners over the next 30 years, then became simply a saloon around the turn of the century.

Of course, the real test is in the taste and the Union Brewery's beer is a special treat. The brew is dark but has a surprisingly sweet and light aftertaste. It's worth a try.

The Union Brewery is located at 28 North C Street in the center of Virginia City. The brewery is open from 3 p.m. to about 3 a.m. (or whenever everyone goes home).

Union Brewery, Virginia City

Virginia City's Real Underground

TALES ABOUT Virginia City's fabulous mines are legendary. The area's gold and silver mines produced in excess of $300 million during the 19 years from 1859 to 1878 — and that was in 19th-century dollars.

Today, the most visible remnants of Virginia City's rich mining past are a handful of decaying wooden headframes and mill foundations, mountains of mine tailings and assorted pieces of mining equipment on display at local museums.

Most of the actual mines that helped finance the Union side in the Civil War and build San Francisco have been abandoned or have collapsed. In fact, just about the only place to find most of the old names and locations of such famous mines as the Ophir, the Gould, the Curry, the Savage and the Yellow Jacket are on faded maps.

There are, however, a couple of places in Virginia City that still provide an opportunity to see and experience what remains of the world's richest mines.

For instance, tours are offered daily from 12 noon to 5 p.m. in the Chollar Mine, located on F Street on the east end of Virginia City. Owners Chris and Penny Kiechler have maintained and restored the entrance and first several hundred yards of the old mine shaft.

Claimed in 1859, the Chollar Mine is one of the oldest in the Comstock Lode. While the mine didn't begin producing ore until 1861, it eventually became the fifth largest in the area in gold and silver production, generating more than $17 million.

The mine, named for Bank of California executive Billy Chollar, was consolidated with another to become the Chollar-Potasi in 1865 and was the first in the region to utilize electric power.

Visitors will get a fascinating glimpse into the underground world of the 19th century miner. The tunnels were small — even today, most visitors over five-and-a-half-feet tall must stoop — and extremely damp. Tour groups must walk on wooden boards to avoid stepping in the oozing Comstock mud.

The Kiechlers are great tour guides and offer a wealth of information about Virginia City's mining industry and history.

During the tour, it is easy to begin to understand the difficulties encountered by the early V.C. miners. Besides the cramped and dark conditions, miners found rock that was difficult to cut — and there always seemed to be hot water seeping from the walls.

The heat and lack of circulating air created serious health hazards that could only be mitigated by blocks of ice that were dropped down into the shafts. Later, many mines installed early versions of air-conditioning systems and other venting devices designed to blow cooler air into the subterranean passages.

The half-hour tour of the Chollar follows the old ore car

tracks. The narrow tunnel opens into a larger underground area that is a fine example of the unique square-set timber system developed on the Comstock to support the tunnels.

The Chollar remains an active mine. The Kiechlers say they periodically chip away the gray-brown rock in the hope of finding some undiscovered pocket of ore overlooked by earlier miners.

There is a $4 fee for adults, $1 fee for children, and children under 4 are free.

A different type of mine tour can be found at the Ponderosa Saloon, located on South C and Taylor streets in Virginia City. The Ponderosa Tunnel was actually dug about ten years ago. This new shaft links the back of the saloon with an old drift of the Best and Belcher, one of the area's oldest mines.

The Best and Belcher was worked in the early 1870s and produced more than $35 million in gold and silver.

The Ponderosa's 20-minute tour, which is admittedly a lot more entertainment than factual, costs $2.50 for adults, $1 for children under 12 and $6 for families.

For more information about the Chollar Mine, call 847-0155. For information about the Ponderosa Mine, call 847-0757.

Chollar Mine, Virginia City

PART III

Reno – Tahoe

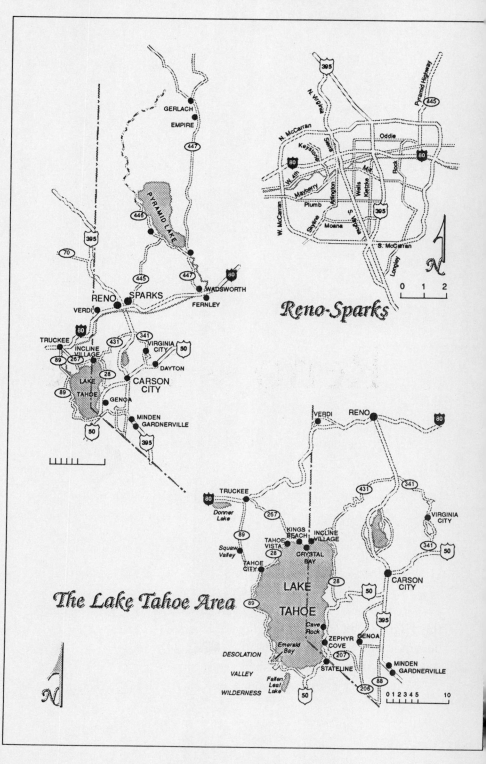

Reno-Sparks

The Lake Tahoe Area

Reno-Tahoe

RENO IS ONE of Nevada's oldest communities and a place that has long held a certain fascination for visitors and, in particular, writers.

As one of the first nationally known legal gambling centers and as the one-time divorce capital of the world, Reno has earned a mystique and reputation that somewhat belie the reality.

Over the years, it has developed an awareness and recognition much beyond its size or relative significance.

Take for instance the words of writer Max Miller, who, in 1941, wrote a book entitled simply, *Reno:*

"Reno sits here upon a river-meadow with her back against the High Sierra and her face toward the Great Desert — and does not care what people say of her.

"Reno has not cared for fifty years. Sixty years.

"She neither affirms nor denies.

"Her living depends on mystery. Her living depends on having people talk about her."

Talk about her they have. And Reno has, over the decades, cultivated its 'Peck's Bad Boy' image.

In the 1930s, Reno Mayor E. E. Roberts made national headlines with his proclamation that, "If I had my way in this Prohibition year, I, as mayor of Reno, would place a barrel of whiskey on every corner, with a dipper, and a sign saying: 'Help yourself, but don't be a hog.'"

Later, in the 1940s and 1950s, when Reno was recognized as the divorce capital of the world, local chamber of commerce officials would toss dime-store rings into the Truckee River to give credibility to all the legends of newly-freed divorcees tossing their old wedding bands into the water in celebration.

Wandering through the self-proclaimed "Biggest Little City in the World," one can still find some of the neighborhoods, buildings and places that molded and shaped Reno.

Additionally, there are newer attractions in the city that are helping the community continue to be a place people talk about.

Meanwhile, in a much different way, Lake Tahoe has also established itself as one of the premier vacation destinations in the west.

With incomparable natural beauty, world-famous ski resorts and plenty of outdoor recreation opportunities, Lake Tahoe is a national treasure and fully deserving of the description once provided it by writer Mark Twain:

"I thought that it must surely be the fairest picture the whole earth affords."

Rediscovering the City of Trembling Leaves (Part 1)

The trees of the Wingfield Park-Court Street region dispense an air of antique melancholy. You become sad and old as you walk under these trees, even on a bright, winter day when all the leaves are gone and the branches make only narrow shadows across homes covered with sunlight...

—Walter Van Tilburg Clark, *City of Trembling Leaves*

HIDDEN JUST BEYOND the bright casino lights and bustling traffic of downtown Reno are the remnants of Walter Van Tilburg Clark's Reno. The Old Reno. The Reno of grand, red and brown brick homes with sidewalks cracked and lifted by the erupting roots of full-grown trees.

There isn't much of the Old Reno remaining. Over the years, the demands of a rapidly growing city have decimated most of the old neighborhoods. However, just minutes from downtown, there exists a handful of streets that have resisted the onslaught of high-rise and parking garages.

A few years ago, the Junior League of Reno prepared a wonderful walking tour brochure of this Old Reno. I recently found my copy and decided to retrace the route of the city's oldest and most historic neighborhood.

Clark's Reno — an area known as the Newlands Heights neighborhood — is roughly bounded by the Truckee River on the north, Flint and Sierra streets on the east, Marsh Avenue on the south and end of California Avenue on the west. Within those boundaries are some of the most important homes ever built in the Truckee Meadows.

The Newlands Heights area is named for Francis G. Newlands, Congressman and U. S. Senator, who built his home and office in the area in 1890. Within a few years, other wealthy citizens followed Newlands' lead and constructed even more majestic homes in the neighborhood.

A good place to begin the tour is at the corner of Arlington and Court streets. (There is a municipal parking lot here.) From here you can either head east on Court to the end of the block or cross Arlington and head toward the heart of the Newlands Heights neighborhood.

Across the way at 247 Court Street is a shaded, shingled house that was built in 1907 by the Frisch family and was home of Roy J. Frisch, a bank cashier who mysteriously disappeared on March 22, 1934, the night before he was to testify in a federal mail fraud case. Legend says that Frisch was murdered by the notorious criminal, "Baby Face" Nelson, reputedly a friend of the man whom Frisch was to testify against.

Two doors down at 219 Court is one of the most significant mansions in the area, the former home of George Wingfield. Built in 1907, the house is an amazing three-story structure highlighted by Doric-style columns and an encircling porch.

Wingfield — called "Prince George" by the media of his day — was perhaps the most powerful man in Nevada at the turn of the century. He controlled most of the banks, many of the mines and nearly all of the politicians.

Head west on Court, across Arlington, and you reach some of the most pleasant and important of the area homes. The house at 401 Court was built in 1913, then purchased in 1921 by Patrick A. McCarran, U. S. Senator from Nevada from 1933 to 1954.

Further down the block at 549 Court is the Sierra Nevada Museum of Art, located in an impressive brick two-story home that incorporates Georgian style architecture and a large front portico with multiple columns. The house was built in 1911 for the Hawkins-Mackay family (descendents of Comstock mining magnate John Mackay) and is one of only a handful in the neighborhood on the National Register of Historic Places.

Just beyond at 617 Court is the former office of Sen. Francis G. Newlands, now converted into a residence, which incorporates Queen Anne-style elements in the design.

A small private drive called Elm Court extends further west to the Newlands home (which is private property).

Adjacent to the Newlands house is one of the most beautiful and unusual homes in the area. Located at 4 Elm Court, this picturesque English-style cottage was built in 1929 by famed Nevada architect Frederic J. DeLongchamps, who designed a number of significant buildings in the state including the downtown Reno post office and the Washoe County Courthouse.

The quaint stone structure, believed to have been DeLongchamps' honeymoon cottage, incorporates a unique hipped roof and has the appearance of belonging in some fairy tale (I've always fantasized that Hobbits live there). It may be my favorite home in the neighborhood.

California Avenue, Reno

Reno's Newlands Heights Neighborhood (Part II)

WALKING THE SHADED Newlands Heights neighborhood, it's easy to imagine you're back in the Reno of a half-century ago. Long before Reno became a place of identical, cookie-cutter subdivisions, condos and townhouses, there was town here with character and individuality, much of which was reflected in the homes of its residents.

Some of the most impressive and historic of Old Reno's homes line California Avenue, overlooking the Truckee River. These were the homes of the power brokers and politicians, the movers, shakers and deal-makers.

Anchoring the east end of the California Avenue homes is the massive George S. Nixon mansion (631 California) built between 1906 and 1911. Nixon was the business associate of U.S. Senator Francis G. Newlands, as well as his seatmate in the U.S. Senate.

Nixon built an incredible home. Resembling an Italian villa, the house boasted 33 rooms, a beautiful tile roof and sculpted hedges. Unfortunately, a fire about seven years ago destroyed portions of the home, and in recent years the estate has been used for storage.

Adjacent to the Nixon home at 657 Ridge Street, is an interesting, Mediterranean-style stucco house built in 1921 by Dr. Cladius West. It was acquired in the 1930s by Dr. Bart Hood. (It is still referred to as the Hood house.)

To the west of the Nixon mansion at 725 California is an elegant home with Mediterranean influences built in 1920 by Dr. Vinton Mueller. The good doctor was married to Mary Ruth Kindler, an actress who starred in the early London productions of J. M Barrie's classic play, Peter Pan. The home was recently restored with a new circular driveway.

Further west at 745 California is a superb example of English Tudor architecture built in the 1930s. Next door at 775 California is a handsome, white, two-story, southern colonial-type home with matching guest house that is perhaps the most striking building on the block.

At the west end of California Avenue (825 California), is a French country-style home built of rusticated stone in the 1920s for Mrs. William Johnston, daughter of Sen. Francis Newlands and granddaughter of Comstock millionaire Sen. William Sharon. Mrs. Johnston later resided in the Nixon mansion, following the death of Sen. Nixon in 1912.

In addition to the Court and Ridge neighborhoods and the mansions overlooking the river, there are other streets lined with equally unique and impressive homes.

In the center of the area is the small, quiet, 2-acre Newlands Circle Park. Land for the park was donated to the city by Sen. Newlands' widow. The park affords a beautiful view of the Truckee River and the teeming city of Reno.

South of the park is Marsh Avenue, another tree-lined street that features some classic examples of bungalows built in the 1920s and 1930s that utilized classic English Tudor and French Provincial country styles.

After completing the mile or so walk through the neighborhood, it becomes very easy to stand in Newlands Circle Park, look out over the city and know why Reno has long been considered such a special place.

> *Perhaps they remember just how they went late one afternoon to Newlands Heights and stood for several hours forgetting dinner while the sun went down over the mountains over toward Verdi and the moon came up and there was the sparkling Truckee at their feet and they felt something they could not put into words, that poets and other such harum-scarum fellows are always trying to put into words...*

— Sherwood Anderson, *So This Is Reno*

DeLongchamps "Honeymoon Cottage," Reno

Downtown Reno

Reno People-Watching

IT'S A COTTON DRESS and short-sleeve summer evening on Virginia Street. A slight breeze carries the ring of slot machine bells mixed with the tinny clang of falling coins.

The famed Reno Arch that stretches across Virginia Street welcomes visitors to the heart of the "Biggest Little City in the World," a slogan the city has proudly worn for more than five decades.

While most of the action can be found at the green felt tables and aisles of shiny slot machines, one of Reno's best — and cheapest — thrills is indulging in that forbidden pleasure that we all deny but secretly enjoy: people watching.

Just about anyone who has ever sat in front of a slot machine mechanically yanking on the handle knows that eventually you get tired and find yourself looking around the room, surveying the surrounding masses.

Over there is a woman in her late 60s with cobalt blue hair, pulling on a slot machine arm with all the intensity of Sylvester Stallone in an arm-wrestling contest.

At an adjacent machine sits a young man wearing jeans, sneakers, a tuxedo cummerbund, pleated white shirt, loosened black bow tie, tux jacket and top hat. Perhaps he's playing basketball at a wedding.

Part of the fun of people-watching — and downtown Reno is prime turf for this kind of thing — is speculating about those being watched.

For example, a well-dressed, olive-skinned man with a pencil-thin mustache (who is probably a visiting plumber from Petaluma) becomes an international jewel thief while a beautiful woman with long blond hair is a budding starlet rather than a hairdresser from Medford, Oregon.

And over there is a large man whose neck is as thick as his head, casually dressed in khakis and a yellow cotton shirt. Surely a professional football player or a bouncer for the casino (actually just an accountant from Fallon).

Of course, people-watching must be subtle. Always carry a pair of dark shades, preferably mirrored. While it can be awkward slipping on a pair of sunglasses inside an already dark room, the shades do allow you the freedom to stare without being noticed.

When sunglasses aren't available, there are other tricks. Leaning your head against an open palm is a good way to look bored while actively scoping out the crowd. Likewise, rubbing your eyes, then kind of glassily looking off in the distance allows most people to think your eyes are tired rather than simply being nosy.

Hats are also a good cover. A baseball cap pulled low over the eyes or a wide-brimmed cowboy hat offer plenty of protection from both the sun and onlookers.

Naturally, the biggest risk of people-watching is that while you are sitting in a dark casino wearing a pair of mirrored sunglasses and a Panama hat, someone else is watching you and speculating that you're a drug dealer from Florida or some TV celebrity. Turnabout is fair play.

National Auto Museum, Reno

Reno is Home of National Automobile Museum

IF EVER there was a project that seemed like it would never be built, it's the National Automobile Museum. But after more than seven years, the museum is open and well worth the wait.

Located on the corner of Lake and Mill streets in Reno, the National Automobile Museum is the result of years of effort by the William F. Harrah Foundation.

The story behind the museum is pretty familiar to those who live in this area. Gaming pioneer Bill Harrah collected more than 1,000 classic and antique cars during his lifetime. Following his death in 1978, his hotels and assets, including the cars, were purchased by Holiday Inns.

In the intervening years, Holiday Inns agreed to donate Harrah's automobile library, valued at $3 million, and 175 vintage cars, valued at more than $18 million, to the non-profit William F. Harrah Foundation created to develop a national automobile museum.

Following a review of 17 locations, the foundation and the Reno Redevelopment Agency selected the Lake and Mill site. For the past five years, the foundation has attempted to arrange for financing for the museum, which was finally accomplished last year.

The new $10 million museum is a marvel. At 105,000 square feet, the facility is said to be the nation's largest museum dedicated exclusively to displaying automobiles. At any time, about 200 of the museum's 240 cars are on display. (The others are rotated into exhibits so each visit to the museum offers something fresh.)

The exterior of the building is unique. Sleek and streamlined like a vintage car, the museum has rounded corners and horizontal chrome strips that highlight the walls, painted, naturally, a 1950s car paint color called heather fire mist.

Inside, the museum features four street scenes. Each represents a period of American development. For instance, the turn-of-the-century street has a simulated dirt road and a blacksmith shop. The 1930s street, paved with brick, includes the facades of a hotel, movie theater and old-time photo shop.

Another scene is the 1950s street, which includes a tract home with a garage where a teenager is working on his car, an auto parts shop and an empty downtown store which has moved to the more profitable suburban malls.

Finally, the modern street hosts a Macy's, an office building, video arcade and park. Each of the streets is lined with appropriate cars, and behind the facades, larger display rooms are filled with the autos of that period.

A multimedia theater presentation, called "The Sizzle," is a good place to start your visit. This film, which you can see in a large theater near the entrance of the museum, orients you to the museum while incorporating unique special effects.

In addition to lots of cars, the museum also has a well-stocked gift store with just about any car-related item you might want to buy. There is also a small restaurant and gaming area. (After all, this is Nevada, and what's a museum without a few slot machines?)

The entrance to the museum fronts the Truckee River, giving it all a very serene feel. A small number of benches are also available for those who just want to sit and enjoy the ambience.

The National Automobile Museum is located on the corner at 10 Lake Street in downtown Reno. Admission is $7.50 for adults, $6.50 for seniors 62 and older, $2.50 for children six to 18, and free for children five and younger. The museum is open 9:30 a.m. to 5:30 p.m. daily except Christmas. For more information, call (702) 333-9300.

Nevada Historical Society, Reno

The Past on Display at the Nevada Historical Society

FOUNDED IN 1904, the Nevada Historical Society in Reno is Nevada's oldest museum. Over the years, the society has accumulated an unparalleled collection of books, writings, photographs and other artifacts that help tell the story of Nevada.

While an excellent library and archives contain much of this material — which, for the most part, can be studied on request — visitors will also find the museum offers one of the best overviews of the history of the state.

Located in a simple square building near the Fleischmann Planetarium, the first indications that this is indeed a repository of the first degree are the ornate bronze doors at the entrance. These green-brown doors, believed to be about a hundred years old, were once part of a private museum that was located in downtown Reno.

Inside the museum exhibits begin with displays about

Nevada's rich Native American history. You can view a replica of a Paiute hut, examine intricate beaded cradleboards and other crafts, and find a half-dozen examples of magnificent willow baskets crafted by the legendary Washo basket-maker, Dat-so-la-lee.

Other displays tell of the great leaders of Nevada's tribes and explain the lifestyle of these fascinating first Nevadans. The section concludes with an exhibit that shows modern-day tribal businesses and development.

From here, you continue into another, larger room which contains displays that tell about the first American explorers to enter what is now Nevada, the discovery of silver and gold on the Comstock Lode in Virginia City and the emergence of Nevada's ranching industry. Here visitors can see antique 19th century furnishings presented as they would have appeared in a typical Reno home and a display containing the famous sack of flour that Reuel Gridley, of Austin, Nev., carried to raise money for the Sanitary Commission (predecessor of the Red Cross) during the Civil War.

The museum also contains an exhibit about the early Reno cycling clubs (complete with authentic, turn-of-the-century bicycle), examples of late 19th century buggy and wagon and a comprehensive display of antique gambling devices and slot machines, including the Liberty Bell, the first three-wheel gaming device.

One of the best ways to view the museum is by joining one of the docent-led tours, which can be arranged by calling ahead for reservations.

The museum also contains a well-stocked gift store with Native American jewelry, gift items and one of the largest selections of books on Nevada topics.

In addition to operating the museum, the Historic Society publishes an excellent quarterly magazine containing scholarly articles about Nevada history, and conducts periodic tours of historic sites in the state.

The Nevada Historical Society is located at 1650 North Virginia Street on the north side of the University of Nevada-Reno campus, just up the street from the Lawlor Events Center and adjacent to the Fleischmann Planetarium. Admission is free, although a $1 donation is suggested. For more information, call 688-1190.

Emerald Bay, Lake Tahoe

Driving Lake Tahoe
(Part 1)

THE DAYS are getting longer and warmer. You notice that your left arm, the one that you always rest in the open window of your car, has taken on a strange color. It almost looks like the start of a tan. Summer is coming.

A great thing about Carson City is that it is only minutes from Lake Tahoe. In fact, I've always wondered why more local businesses don't promote themselves by pointing out their proximity to the lake and developing cooperative programs with ski resorts and businesses up there.

To reach Lake Tahoe, travel south of Carson City on U.S. Highway 50. About two miles south of town, follow Highway 50 as it heads west through the mountains. Continue west until you spot the lake, then turn south on Highway 50 toward Stateline.

At 6,000 feet above sea level, Lake Tahoe is a great place to escape the summer heat, and one of the best ways to enjoy the lake is to take the 72-mile drive around the lake.

No matter how many times you cross Spooner Summit from Carson City, your first glimpse of the lake is inspiring. Stretched out before you is a placid sheet of clear, blue water surrounded by magnificent alpine scenery. Writer Mark Twain called it the "fairest picture the whole earth affords."

Just below Spooner Summit, the road branches south to Stateline and Zephyr Cove or north to Incline Village, Crystal Bay and Tahoe City. On this day, we headed south.

The road passes through Glenbrook, an historic community that was the site of Lake Tahoe's first resort, in 1863. Glenbrook was also the location of an active timber industry for many decades.

Further on is famous Cave Rock, where the highway passes through 75 feet of stone. The rock was a sacred spot for the Washo Indians, the original inhabitants of Lake Tahoe, who would place their dead in the waters below the distinctive rock.

A few miles further is Zephyr Cove, home of the M.S. Dixie paddlewheeler, a fine beach and a rustic old-style lodge. Additionally, visitors can enjoy horseback riding on the adjacent hillsides.

Just ahead is Stateline. In addition to being the boundary between Nevada and California, Stateline is also where most of the Tahoe action can be found. A half-dozen high-rise hotel-casinos sit at the south end of the lake, offering good times, including name entertainment.

While most people enjoy the gaming fun at Stateline, those who prefer simpler pleasures will also find plenty of things to do. For example, a new club, Bill's, offers 10-cent popcorn and a delicious chocolate store. One of my weaknesses is video games, and few places offer as large a selection of games as Harrah's.

Beyond Stateline is South Lake Tahoe. The highway is lined with motels and hotels, but off to the right you can still view the loveliest lake in the world. An interesting side trip is to the Heavenly Valley Tram. For a few bucks, you can rise to 2,000 feet above the lake, then relax and dine at the Top-of-the-Tram restaurant. The view is incredible.

About 15 miles from Stateline, you finally pass out of the heaviest development around the lake and head north on Highway 89. Here there are several great beaches — El Dorado, Regan and Pope — and the Pope-Baldwin Recreation Area.

The recreation area includes an Historic Estates Tour, during which you can wander through several mansions, some more than a century old. The homes have been restored to their former splendor and provide a glimpse of the lifestyles of the rich-and-famous before they were discovered by Robin Leach.

The Lake Tahoe Visitors Center, located in the area, is also a good place to stop to learn about the history, flora and fauna of Lake Tahoe. From here you can also follow an interpretive nature trail or, during the right time of year, view giant salmon traveling through a Stream Profile Chamber to spawn upstream.

The views on the road now are spectacular as it winds through the mountains above the southwestern edge of the lake. At this time of year at Eagle Falls, you can actually drive over a waterfall — it's really a beautiful sight and makes for a good photo.

Just beyond the waterfall is Emerald Bay. Often called the most photographed place in the world, it's easy to see why people flock to this part of the lake.

Emerald Bay is an amazing place. Park at the overlook and climb on the rocks above the bay to get a good overview of both the bay and Eagle Falls. Below you can see Fannette Island, the only island in Lake Tahoe. The small stone building on the island is the Tea House, built by Lora Knight, who also constructed Vikingsholm, the 39-room Scandinavian mansion at the head of the bay.

Emerald Bay is a great place to spend a few hours. Tours of Vikingsholm are available and the scenery is wonderful. Twain was right about this place.

Sand Harbor, Lake Tahoe

Tahoe Touring
(Part 2)

TAHOE. There is an old Washo Indian legend that says the lake was named for a young brave who fought and killed a terrible monster, called the Ong, that lived in the lake.

According to the story, the Ong had an evil human face, giant wings, webbed feet and massive armored scales that couldn't be pierced by spears and arrows. This horrible fiend lived at the bottom of the lake and loved to surface, then search for sustenance in the form of human flesh.

The young brave hoped to prove his courage by allowing the Ong to capture him, then shooting poisoned arrows into the creature's mouth. His ploy was successful and the Ong died. Tahoe survived and in addition to having the lake named for him, captured the heart of the Chief's daughter.

All of this leads us to the second half of our tour of Lake Tahoe. In the last chapter, we concentrated on the southern end of the lake, including Zephyr Cove, Stateline, South Lake Tahoe and Emerald Bay.

Next stop is Bliss State Park. Located a few miles from the turnout for Emerald Bay and Vikingsholm, Bliss Park is a perfect spot for photographing the clear, deep blue depths of Rubicon Bay. In addition to hiking trails and some outrageously wonderful scenery, there is also a fairly secluded but highly recommended beach and a picnic area.

A few miles further is Meeks Bay, where you will find another great beach and a camping ground. About three miles north is Sugar Pine Point State Park, another of California's fine facilities on Tahoe. Here you will find some incredible views of the lake in both directions. The park also includes the Ehrmann Mansion, which was used in filming *The Godfather Part II,* and an extremely pretty picnic area (where you can imagine you are enjoying the buffet at Michael Corleone's son's first communion party).

From here it is about seven miles to Tahoe City, one of the most commercial spots on the north shore. Despite the development, Tahoe City has some fine places to eat and shop. In addition, during the summer and late spring, it is the place where you can rent a raft to float down the Truckee River.

Since Tahoe City is the outlet for the Truckee (which is the only river that drains from the lake; it ends at Pyramid Lake) it is also the site of Fanny Bridge, where you can actually see some large trout spilling out the lake and into the river.

From Tahoe City, you can travel northwest on Highway 89 to the town of Truckee by following the river. Along the way, you can also find Squaw Valley, the site of the 1960 Winter Olympics.

You can also continue traveling around the lake by heading northeast on Highway 28. Along the way you'll pass through the hamlets of Carnelian Bay (another fairly developed community with plenty of restaurants and businesses), Tahoe Vista and King's Beach. There is a fine public beach at King's Beach.

Crystal Bay is the northern border between California and Nevada on the lake. Not surprisingly, you'll find a number of hotel-casinos offering the famous Nevada-style fun (our euphemism for gambling), including the renovated Tahoe Biltmore. (It's been redone in a classic art deco style.) The revamped Cal-Neva Club, once owned by Frank Sinatra and famous for its swimming pool, is half in Nevada and half in California.

Three miles further is Incline Village, which has a number of businesses, restaurants and a couple of the world's most beautiful golf courses. A few miles outside of Incline Village is the Ponderosa Ranch, film site for the long-running *Bonanza* TV show and, more recently, site of the shooting of *Bonanza: The Next Generation.*

In addition to serving as a movie set, the Ponderosa is also a western-theme amusement park with hayrides, barbecues, gift and crafts shops and horseback rides.

Just south of the Ponderosa is Nevada's Lake Tahoe State Park, offering one of the most beautiful beaches at the lake at Sand Harbor. You can also find a boat launch.

About 10 miles further south is the intersection with U.S. Highway 50, where you can bid adieu to the lake and return to Carson City.

For more information on Lake Tahoe, contact the Lake Tahoe Visitors Authority, Box 16299, South Lake Tahoe, CA 95706, (916) 544-5050.

Cave Rock, Lake Tahoe

The Other Side
of Cave Rock

MOST OF US only know of Cave Rock as the tunnel we travel through when heading south from Glenbrook to Zephyr Cove on the eastern shore of Lake Tahoe.

But there's much more to the story of this famous Tahoe landmark. History records that the first mention of the rock formation was in 1855 when pioneer surveyor George H. Goddard described it as a "Legendary Cave."

Presumably he used this description to reflect the importance the cave had to the native Washo Indians in the area. One Washo legend has it that the enemies of their tribe were imprisoned in the cave by the god of the world, and that you could still hear their cries and moans.

Of course, today we are forced to only imagine what the cave was like, because it was obliterated about 75 years ago when a 200-foot tunnel was carved through the back of it to create the present Cave Rock tunnel. You can see the "cave" part of the tunnel if you look at the rough rock walls that constitute the last couple of hundred feet of the southbound or western tunnel.

A hike around the imposing rock, however, still provides glimpses of the past. For example, to the immediate west you can still find the remains of the original Lake Bigler Toll Road that circled Cave Rock.

In the mid-1860s, a one-mile road costing some $40,000 was constructed around the rock. When it was built, this section was the most expensive stretch of road between Placerville and Washoe City.

During a recent visit, I could see the first quarter-mile or so of the road, including the hand-chiseled stone buttresses. At the western-most point — where the road apparently veered out over the lake and was supported by a 100-foot trestle bridge — you can peer down to the rocks and water below and understand why the tunnel was built.

Additionally, from the southern side, you can see several smaller caves in the granite rock. One, located above the median between the north and southbound traffic lanes, is actually fairly large and, if you listen hard, you can hear the wind whistling through it — or perhaps it was the faint wailing of the lost enemies of the Washo tribe.

From the north side, you can also see several shapes in the rock face below the tunnel that have been given names, including, just above the water, the 50-foot profile of the "Lady of the Lake" (complete with eyelashes) and the "Gorilla Profile," located on the upper curve of the rock.

Cave Rock is also the location of one of the Nevada Division of State Parks more popular boating and fishing spots. Visitors will find a boat launch ramp, restrooms and a pleasant, small sandy beach area with room for swimming or catching a few rays of sunlight.

There is a $4 day use fee for parking at Cave Rock and using the state park facilities. The pass is also good during the day for the state park system's two other Lake Tahoe recreational areas; Sand Harbor, near Incline Village, and Spooner Lake.

Cave Rock is located about 20 miles west of Carson City via U.S. Highway 50. For more information about the state park facilities, contact the Lake Tahoe Nevada State Park, 2005 Highway 28, Incline Village, NV 89450, 831-0494.

M.S. Dixie

Paddle-Wheelers
Call Tahoe Home

IN HIS BOOK *Roughing It,* writer Mark Twain wrote of Lake Tahoe: "So singularly clear was the water that where it was only 20 or 30-feet deep the bottom was so perfectly distinct that the boat seemed floating in the air . . . so empty and airy did all spaces seem below us, and so strong was the sense of floating high aloft in mid-nothingness that we called these boat-excursions, 'balloon-voyages.'"

Twain was correct in saying that probably the best way to experience Lake Tahoe is from a boat floating across the lake's crystal-clear surface. On a typical day, with the sun overhead and a slight breeze, there are few places as breathtakingly beautiful as Lake Tahoe.

A great "balloon voyage" is traveling across the lake on one of the two paddle-wheelers that call Lake Tahoe home.

One, the *M.S. Dixie,* is docked at Zephyr Cove, located

about 35 miles from Carson City via Highway 50 over Spooner Summit. The *M.S. Dixie,* which is more than 60 years old, has been sailing on Lake Tahoe since 1972.

Originally a Mississippi cotton barge, the *M.S. Dixie* has been renovated into a majestic 360-passenger sternwheeler with two enclosed decks, two full-service bars, a dining room, dance floor and a glass bottom.

The view from any of her two decks is spectacular and, in those portions of the lake where the water is so blue and clear, the effect is of floating on a huge riverboat in the sky.

During the year, the *M.S. Dixie* offers a variety of excursion tours on the lake. The Historic Glenbrook Breakfast Cruise is a two-hour ride on the lake that includes fresh coffee and a full breakfast.

The 2-½-hour Emerald Bay Cruise is the most scenic as the boat slips into beautiful Emerald Bay and by Vikingsholm Castle. Other cruises include a tour of the bright lights and excitement of South Shore, a Sunset Dinner Dance cruise and a Champagne Brunch.

The *M.S. Dixie's* California counterpart is docked at the Ski Run Marina on Lake Tahoe's South Shore. The *Tahoe Queen* is a marvelous replica of an authentic Mississippi riverboat.

Built in the early 1980s, the *Tahoe Queen* is the largest cruise ship on the lake and can accommodate 500 passengers. The *Tahoe Queen* is fitted with twin paddle-wheels and, like the *M.S. Dixie,* has two enclosed lower decks and an open upper deck.

Inside, the elegant ship features plenty of oak and brass as well as a glass bottom for viewing under the surface of the lake. Passengers will find a fine ship's gallery that prepares food ranging from hotdogs to salads. At night, the dinner cruise can include prime rib or halibut.

The *Tahoe Queen* embarks on daily two-hour daytime cruises and a three-hour sunset dinner ride with live music.

The cruises all follow the same route to Emerald Bay.
For *M.S. Dixie* information or reservations, call 588-3508. For
Tahoe Queen information or reservations, call (916) 541-3364.

Pyramid Lake

Pyramid Lake Makes Impression on Viewers

We encamped on the shore, opposite a very remarkable rock in the lake, which had attracted our attention for many miles. It rose, according to our estimate, 600 feet above the water; and, from the point we viewed it, presented a pretty exact outline of the great pyramid of Cheops...I called it Pyramid Lake...

—John C. Fremont

IT'S SOMEHOW APPROPRIATE that explorer John C. Fremont thought of ancient Egypt when he first saw Pyramid Lake. Like the pyramids, there is a timeless, mysterious quality to this hauntingly beautiful desert lake.

Pyramid Lake, which has more than 70 miles of beaches, is located 33 miles north of Reno. You can either travel north of Reno on State Route 445 or go east on Interstate 80 to

Wadsworth, then turn north on State Route 447 to Nixon.

When you glimpse Pyramid Lake, it's easy to understand why it made such an impression on Fremont. Surrounded by high desert, the lake seems to burst into your awareness.

Fremont described his first sighting of the lake by saying it "broke upon our eyes like the ocean." Part of the special feel one gets from the lake is that it is, literally, a desert oasis.

Pyramid Lake is the largest remnant of ancient Lake Lahontan, a giant inland sea that once covered most of Nevada. The lake receives a regular flow of water from the winding Truckee River, which begins at Lake Tahoe. The lake is also the center of the 322,000 acre Pyramid Lake Paiute Reservation.

When Fremont stumbled upon the lake, he also found it teeming with large fish, noting, "their flavor was excellent — superior, in fact, to that of any fish I have ever known."

Over the years, the fish have remained important to the lake and its people. Fishing enthusiasts have long sought the great Lahontan cutthroat trout at Pyramid. The world record for a cutthroat trout was established in 1925 at Pyramid Lake.

The lake is also famous as home of the rare cui-ui, a fish that first appeared more than 2 million years ago. Today, the fish is an endangered species protected by the U.S. government.

A trip to Pyramid Lake is a fun day trip. In addition to fishing and the lake's stark beauty, the area is an historic treasure.

Stop at the historical marker located on Highway 447, south of Nixon, to learn about the "Battle Born" state's most famous skirmish, the so-called Pyramid Lake War of 1860.

The battle was sparked by growing resentment among the Paiutes about the large numbers of white miners and settlers not respectful of the land or the native people, who were crossing through the area on their way to California and Virginia City's wealthy gold and silver fields.

A series of confrontations and skirmishes was followed by the discovery of three (or four or five, depending on reports of the day) men found dead at a trading post on the Carson River. Word quickly spread of an Indian uprising, despite evidence the murders may have been in retaliation for the men kidnapping some Paiute women.

A small force of 105 men, largely miners and merchants from Carson City and Virginia City, was formed to seek revenge on any Paiutes unlucky enough to be in its path.

On May 12, 1860, the volunteer army marched from the location of present-day Wadsworth, along the banks of the Truckee River, toward Pyramid Lake.

But the Paiutes received word of the advancing hoard and prepared an ambush. More than half of the army died in the fight, including Major Ormsby, the unofficial leader of the group (and later namesake of Ormsby County, now part of Carson City).

The battle encouraged a major panic, and a much larger and better-organized force was gathered to seek retribution. About two weeks after the first battle, a far larger army was marshalled, which included more than 750 regular U.S. Army soldiers from California.

This time, the heavily-outnumbered native warriors suffered more substantial losses, an estimated 40 to 50 dead, while the militia had three dead and five wounded. The second battle effectively ended any large-scale battles between the Paiutes and the increasing number of white settlers.

Another historic marker on State Route 445, west of Sutcliffe, describes the discovery of Pyramid Lake and the history of the area.

The hillsides surrounding the lake contain several sites with petroglyphs, which are Indian rock writing. One location, south of Nixon and not far off State Route 447, has some particularly fine drawings depicting the sun and a warrior.

Additionally, the lake is a fine spot for picnicking, camping, boating, water-skiing, swimming, hiking and exploring — but don't forget you need a tribal permit from the Pyramid Lake Tribe Ranger Station if you want to fish, camp or use your boat.

On the east side of the lake is Warrior Point Park, nine miles north of Sutcliffe. The park has picnic tables and camping sites.

The lake's unique rock formations, including the famous Pyramid, are tufa formations made of calcium carbonate deposits. You can find many fascinating shapes on the shores of the lake.

Tours are available of the Pyramid Lake Fisheries, located in Sutcliffe on the southwest side of the lake. The fishery operates an extensive fishery restoration program, and is responsible for planting millions of fish each year into the lake.

Anaho Island, adjacent to Pyramid rock, is home for thousands of American white pelicans. The island, off limits to boats, is one of only eight white pelican nesting grounds in North America. It also serves as a nesting station for California gulls (yes, seagulls in Nevada), double-crested cormorants, blue herons and terns.

For more information, contact the Pyramid Lake Fisheries, Sutcliffe, 89510, 673-6335 or the Pyramid Lake Paiute Tribe Ranger Station, Sutcliffe, 89510, 476-0132.

Palomino Valley's
Wild Horses

WILD HORSES are synonymous with Nevada and one of the best places to see these magnificent creatures up close is the Palomino Valley Wild Horse and Burro Placement Center, north of Sparks.

While nothing can compare to actually seeing a band of wild horses racing across the wide-open range land of central Nevada, at the Palomino Center you can get to within a few feet of these elusive phantoms of the purple sage.

Operated by the Bureau of Land Management, the Palomino Center is a series of corrals and pens that can accommodate as many as 500 wild horses and burros (although there are usually about fifty on the premises). While its main purpose is to house the animals prior to adoption, it also is a good place to learn something about wild horses and burros.

While there are several theories about the introduction of the horse to the American West, most experts agree that today's wild horses and burros are descendents of animals who were either abandoned or escaped into the wilderness over the last century.

Over the years, wild horses in particular have acquired a romantic image. They are the untamed, free spirits of the American West, made famous in dozens of books, including Will James' *Smoky*, about a Nevada mustang.

Today, the BLM estimates there are as many as 20,000 wild horses in Nevada, most living in the foothills, canyons and valleys of central and northern Nevada where food and water is available.

A few of the best places in this area to spot wild horses are in the foothills outside of Dayton and Mound House and in the valleys north of Virginia City and south of Interstate 80. There are also thousands of wild horses in the valleys around Austin, Eureka and Tonopah.

Of course, one of the best things about the Palomino Center is that you don't have to go driving around the state hoping to spot a band of wild horses. Another nice aspect is that the BLM staff offers guided tours of the facilities upon request.

Jeff Weeks, assistant manager of the Palomino Center, points out that there are a few misconceptions about wild horses. For instance, some people believe a wild horse cannot be trained. Weeks said they can be domesticated, if properly trained at a relatively young age, and can make excellent ranch and show horses.

He notes that three palominos have been trained at the Palomino Center by staff and became part of the U.S. Marine Mountain Color Guard stationed in Barstow, California. He said the three have appeared in numerous parades, including at the Fiesta Bowl, the Reno Rodeo Parade and the Virginia City Camel Race Parade.

During my recent visit, I watched with fascination as one BLM staffer explained how he gained the trust of a wild horse.

He walked into a pen with a horse that had only been in the center for two weeks. He explained how to watch for the telltale body language that indicates the horse feels threatened and will attack.

Within a few minutes, with only patience and soft words, he had calmed the horse and was scratching it on the nose.

For anyone interested in adopting a wild horse, the BLM staff can help in explaining the process. Essentially, a potential adopter must prove to the BLM that he or she has proper facilities for the animal, then must pay a $125 fee. The adopter also agrees to maintain the horse for one year, after which time the BLM will turn over title to the animal, provided the horse has been given good care.

Weeks says that there are only a handful of placement centers throughout the U.S. and the Palomino Center is the main processing facility for Nevada, which is home to the largest number of wild horses in the country.

As for horses too old to be trained and therefore unlikely to be adopted, Weeks said that they are shipped to "horse sanctuaries" located in South Dakota and on the Oklahoma/Kansas border. "They are a kind of retirement home for the horses," he said.

The Palomino Valley Wild Horse and Burro Placement Center is located about 15 miles north of Sparks on the Pyramid Lake Highway (State Route 445). The center is open from 8 a.m. to 4 p.m., Monday through Friday, except holidays. For more information, call 673-1150.

Wild horses, Palomino Valley

Black Rock Desert

Found in Gerlach: Wagon Trails and Fine Ravioli

FOR A SMALL STATE, Nevada is blessed with an unusually wide choice of eating experiences. Because of its world-famous hotel-casinos, there are many fine restaurants throughout the state that can accommodate every budget or desired cuisine.

However, one of the real pleasures about exploring the rural parts of the state is discovering some out-of-the-way special eatery. Hidden far off the main roads — long away from the plastic sameness of fast food chains — are a handful of unique places to eat, such as the eclectically-named "Bruno's Country Club" in Gerlach.

Located about an hour-and-a-half north of Reno on State Route 447, Gerlach sits on the edge of the Black Rock Desert. In fact, while traveling on the road through the high desert to Gerlach, it's good to remind yourself that you're not heading to the end of the world — it only seems that way.

Seriously, the trip is straight and fast, particularly if you're dreaming about Bruno's special dish, the most incredible ravioli you will ever find.

Now, to many people, a ravioli is a doughy square filled with a nameless, barely edible green paste that is covered by a runny, red tomato sauce. Far too often, restaurant ravioli have been frozen into mediocrity and soaked in canned sauce.

But at Bruno's, the ravioli are an art form. Owner Bruno Selmi, who is ably assisted by members of his family, uses a round wine glass to cut the dough (none of this square stuff), which results in a uniquely round ravioli.

Inside each rotund dumpling, which are made fresh daily, are specially-seasoned ground meats, cheese and herbs. Likewise the sauce is rich and thick, oozing with flavor and fine Italian smells.

Perhaps the most impressive thing about Bruno's ravioli are their size. These babies are huge. Anyone can eat one of them, and most can handle two, but three is a challenge, and four is tempting fate and the limits of your stomach.

Rumor has it that a man once ate five, got lost in the Black Rock Desert for a month — and still wasn't hungry when he was found.

Non-ravioli fans, however, will also discover that Bruno makes a pretty good cheeseburger with large fries.

In addition to Bruno's, Gerlach is the gateway to the Black Rock Desert. In the 1840s, the desert was part of the famed Lassen-Applegate Trail, one of the main wagon routes used by settlers heading to Oregon and northern California.

These hardy immigrants would veer from the Humboldt River corridor outside of Winnemucca, then head west into the desert, searching for a triangular mountain called Black Rock, which served as a compass point.

From there, they would follow the base of the mountains, traveling from spring to spring, including many hot springs (imagine drinking from a sulfur-saturated, tepid pool) before passing through a place called High Rock Canyon.

As a result of the historic significance of this trail, the Lassen-Applegate has been considered for inclusion in a national system of historic trails by the National Park Service.

Hikers who travel to High Rock Canyon can find places along the historic trail where wagon wheels have cut grooves in the rock. An excellent source of information for hiking in the region is *Hiking the Sierra Nevada*, by John Hart, published by Sierra Club Books.

Gerlach is also famous as the home of the renowned "Planet X" pottery studio. Planet X owner John Bogard has created a national reputation as a fine potter with his beautiful and ornate, handmade pots and dishes. Many of his designs incorporate the surrounding landscape.

To reach the studio, which sits amidst some rather unique landscaping, travel east of Gerlach on Highway 81, then turn onto a dirt road that is marked "Planet X."

Of course, the Black Rock Desert does much to define Gerlach. Nearby is the site where the world land speed record of 633.468 miles per hour was set by British racer Richard Noble in 1983. Additionally, the surrounding desert is popular for dirt-biking and land-sailing (wind-sailing on a board with wheels).

For more information about Bruno's Country Club, call 557-2220. For information about Planet X, call 557-2500.

Train from Truckee (Courtesy of AMTRAK)

Riding the Rails through the Sierra Nevada

THERE'S SOMETHING SPECIAL about riding on a train. Sure, it's usually cheaper and faster to take your car or an airplane to travel from place to place, but there's nothing quite like a train ride.

When we are near a train, there are so many familiar sounds and smells. The sound of the locomotive as it breathes, the strong smell of its diesel lifeblood, the high-pitched squeal as it slows to a stop and, of course, the loud blare of its whistle — these are what a train is all about.

Trains conjure up images of a more genteel time, when life in the fast lane meant walking quickly, and only matches suffered from burnout.

Fortunately, in the Reno-Lake Tahoe area, there is a unique opportunity to enjoy the sensations of riding a train and viewing incredible scenery — without having to actually travel too far.

Amtrak, which operates the nation's railroads, offers a remarkably inexpensive opportunity to travel on a train from Reno to Truckee. Once a day, passengers can climb aboard a modern diesel train at the downtown Reno depot, then sit back and enjoy a ride through some of Nevada's and California's most beautiful scenery.

Much of the train route parallels the Truckee River, offering some amazing views. On your one side, you can watch as the crisp, clear waters of the Truckee rush by, while on the other, lush, green mountains rise from the river canyon to form spectacular peaks.

You pass through little towns that you never really notice when zooming by in a car, such as Floriston, Farad and Verdi. The latter, besides being one of Nevada's most picturesque little communities, was also the site of the first train robbery in the west, in 1870.

From the train, you can also see the aging wooden flumes that once carried logs that were made into lumber for the California market. Verdi was also one of the main collection and storage points for winter ice, which was sold to California's valley and coastal towns in the summer months.

From here, the track meanders across the California-Nevada border, through miles of peaceful mountain scenery. The process of riding on a train can be cathartic, helping to clear out from one's head the clutter and refuse of everyday pressures.

Almost before you know it, the train is nearing Truckee. While only about an hour has passed, you feel like you've been away from your normal life for at least a day.

For those with more time on their hands, continue from Truckee down to Sacramento. The trip, which takes about four hours from Reno, offers equally breathtaking scenery as you travel over Donner Summit, then pass through the heart of the Sierra Nevada before dropping down into the Sierra foothills and Sacramento Valley.

Amtrak offers one trip daily from Reno to Truckee. The train departs from Reno at 8:34 a.m. and arrives in Truckee at 9:27 a.m. The return trip departs at 5:48 p.m. and arrives in Reno at 6:41 p.m.

A roundtrip ticket for an adult is $21, although Amtrak has a reasonable family package which allows one adult to travel for $21, a spouse to travel for $10.50 and each child (ages 2-11) to travel for $2.75 each (children under 2 are free).

The trip from Reno to Sacramento costs $50 one-way or $75-100 roundtrip (depending on whether you travel on a discount rate). Of course, all prices quoted here are subject to change.

For more information, contact Amtrak at 1-800-872-7245.

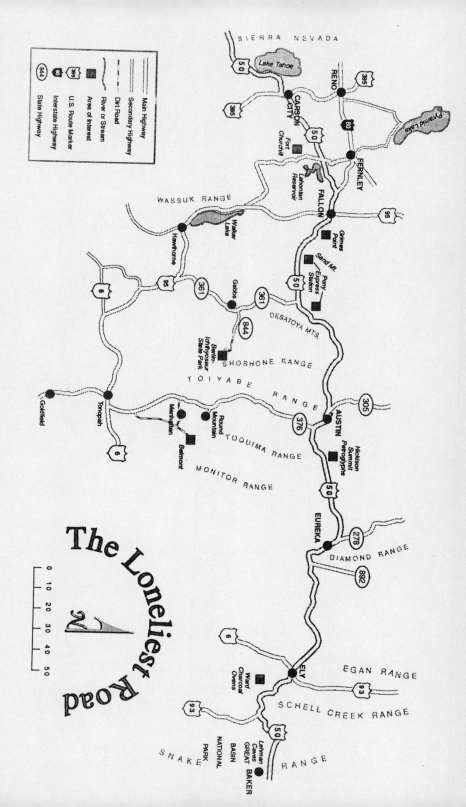

PART IV

The
Loneliest
Road

U.S. Highway 50

The Loneliest Road

"It's totally empty," says an AAA counselor. "There are no points of interest. We don't recommend it." The 287-mile stretch of U.S. 50, running from Ely to Fernley, Nev., passes nine towns, two abandoned mining camps, a few gas pumps and an occasional coyote. "We warn all motorists not to drive there," says the AAA rep, "unless they're confident of their survival skills."

— *Life* magazine, *July 1986*

I LOVE HIGHWAY 50. In a world where most highways are either gridlocked with cars for much of the day or lined for miles and miles with copy-cat fast food joints, Highway 50 is unique.

Highway 50 is the American West. It is open cattle range, red-violet skies, wide valleys that stretch off as far as you can see and mountains pinched and lined like an old rancher's face. It is

143

mining towns seemingly bypassed by the changes of modern society and the tumbled-down stone ruins of a Pony Express station.

Highway 50 has been called the Loneliest Road in America because there aren't a lot of towns or people on the 300-plus-mile ribbon of asphalt that traverses the width of Nevada. It is lonely and it is beautiful.

There are about a half-dozen towns along the route, in which a traveler can find gas stations, restaurants, grocery stores, motels and hotels. But there also is a lot of elbow-room between these towns, usually sixty or seventy miles.

The communities are each special and distinct. At the far-eastern end is the tiny hamlet of Baker, gateway to the Great Basin National Park. An hour up the road is Ely, a former copper mining town that has survived the loss of its major industry and resurrected its historic Nevada Northern Railway as a living museum and excursion railroad.

Another hour or so away is Eureka, a well-preserved, late 19th century mining town. Austin, seventy miles farther west, was once the most important city in the state, after Virginia City, and still boasts several of the most historic churches in Nevada.

Fallon is one of the state's most important agricultural areas and home of the Fallon Naval Station, a top training ground for the nation's best pilots. Dayton, near the west side of the state, is one of the state's first towns and an important part of the famous Comstock mining district.

Much of Highway 50 was once part of the legendary Pony Express trail, which has spawned hundreds of books, stories, television shows and movies, despite its relatively short, 18-month history. Later, the route was part of the Overland Stagecoach road and, in the early part of this century, incorporated into the Lincoln Highway, America's first transcontinental highway.

The following pieces only touch on the wealth of history and legend that surround Highway 50, America's loneliest and most historic road.

Surviving America's Lonely Highway 50

THE ROAD WAS EMPTY in either direction. Above, the setting sun cast an orange glow that made the clouds look like huge cotton balls that had been dipped in iodine. Welcome to Highway 50, the so-called loneliest road in America.

In July 1986, *Life* magazine described Nevada's Highway 50 from Ely to Fernley as the "loneliest road" in America. *Life* said that there were no attractions or points of interest along the 287-mile stretch of road and recommended drivers have "survival skills" to travel the route.

"We didn't agree with that," said Ferrel Hansen, director of the White Pine Chamber of Commerce in Ely. "But rather than just get mad and forget about it, we decided to have some fun with it."

Hansen said the communities along the route developed a tongue-in-cheek "Highway 50 Survival Kit." The kit contained brochures and maps detailing places along the route and a special Highway 50 map, which travelers can have validated in the five largest communities (Ely, Eureka, Austin, Fallon and Fernley). Validated maps are redeemed for a Highway 50 bumper sticker and a "Silver State Survivor" certificate.

Additionally, the Nevada State Legislature authorized Highway 50, "Loneliest Road in America," road signs to be erected along the route.

Since then, Highway 50 has been featured on the network news and in newspapers and magazines across the country. More than 10,000 Highway 50 Survival Kits have been distributed and traffic counts show that the road isn't quite as lonely as it used to be.

Of course, Hansen points out that the promotion succeeded because, contrary to *Life* magazine's opinion, Highway 50 is one of the most historic and scenic routes in the west.

The road roughly parallels the trail blazed a century ago by the brave Pony Express riders. Later, Highway 50 was originally part of the Lincoln Highway, the first intercontinental road in the U.S. Stretching the width of Nevada, the road is a pathway through places seemingly untouched by man.

It passes through a land where watch-for-cattle signs far outnumber pedestrian-crossing warnings. Cowboys here are the genuine article — the dust on their boots, the smell on their clothes and stains on their hatbands were earned.

Starting at the Utah-Nevada border, the traveler heading west on Highway 50 reaches mighty Wheeler Peak, the crown jewel of America's newest national park, the Great Basin National Park. Within the park, visitors will find Lehman Caves, an extensive series of fascinating limestone caverns at the base of Wheeler Peak.

Additionally, the park is home of several of the west's largest and oldest groves of Bristlecone Pines. These gnarled trees, which are the oldest living things, can grow in the most inhospitable of climates. Many in the park are more than 3,000 years old.

About an hour from the park is Ely, an historic copper-mining town that is also home of the Nevada Northern Railway Museum, often called one of the best-preserved shortline railroads in the country.

The road between Ely and Eureka — some 77 miles long — affords an opportunity to experience some of Nevada's unique high desert scenery. This is open range so be careful of the cattle that often roam freely across the highway.

The open road offers time for introspection. Sometimes there is no other traffic as far as you can see in either direction. Out here, one can begin to comprehend the loneliness of the cowboy searching for strays or the Pony Express rider galloping into the unknown.

The next town is Eureka, perhaps the best example of a 19th century mining town in the state. Eureka is a great place to explore, with its fascinating ruins and beautifully restored historic buildings, including the county courthouse, built in 1879, and the *Eureka Sentinel* newspaper building, now a museum.

About 45 miles west of Eureka is Hickison Summit, the site of rare Indian petroglyphs, which are ancient Indian rock writings.

Austin, which is just ahead, is another former mining town that still claims three of the loveliest frontier churches in the west, several cemeteries and a number of historic structures and ruins.

From Austin, it is a two hour drive to Fallon. Along the way are the ruins of several Pony Express and Overland Stage stations. The best preserved are the stone ruins at Cold Springs and those near Sand Mountain, which is an unusual 600-foot tall mound of sand popular with off-roaders.

About fifteen minutes from Fallon is another Indian petroglyph site at Grimes Point. An interpretive trail leads through the writings. Adjacent to the petroglyphs is Hidden Cave, an archaeological site that has yielded important artifacts that tell the story of Nevada's earliest inhabitants.

The Churchill County Museum in Fallon is one of the finest rural museums in the state. Among its exhibits are excellent displays describing the hardships of traveling by wagon train across Nevada. A few miles from Fallon is the Lahontan Reservoir, which offers a full range of water sports.

An interesting sidetrip just south of the loneliest road, on U.S. 95, is historic Fort Churchill. The facility was built in 1861 as a garrison for federal troops.

About a half-hour from Fort Churchill is Fernley, the western gateway to the loneliest road. Originally an important agricultural center and railroad station, Fernley has evolved into a quiet small town that offers plenty of services for road travelers on either Highway 50 or Interstate 80.

Turning from Highway 50 (it is actually Alternate Highway 50 that runs through Fernley — but what do you expect from a magazine located in New York City!) onto busy Interstate 80, one cannot help but notice the differences between the roads. If Interstate 80 can be described as a sprint, than Highway 50 is a casual jog. There's something to be said for loneliness.

For more information, contact the White Pine Chamber of Commerce, (702) 289-8877.

The Mood and Magic
of Fort Churchill

THERE IS A PEACEFULNESS at Fort Churchill. The wind blows quietly through the zebra-striped quaking aspens that grow along the nearby Carson River and the afternoon shadows paint broad strokes across the tan adobe ruins.

Fort Churchill, located 40 miles east of Carson City via U.S. 50 and Alternate U.S. 93, is one of western Nevada's most photogenic locales. Photographers find the fort a continually changing canvas. The time-worn ruins of the fort take on new shapes and moods depending on the light at different times of the day.

The picturesque fort was built in 1860 by the U.S. Army to provide a home for a garrison of troops that would protect western Nevada settlers, who feared an Indian uprising.

Earlier that year, local tribes had fought with the white settlers in the so-called Pyramid Lake War. The dispute apparently was started after three white men kidnapped and held prisoner two Indian women at a trading post called Williams Station, located about 30 miles east of Carson City.

The Indians responded by attacking the station, burning its buildings and freeing the women.

Stories about the raid began to circulate — and, naturally, became exaggerated at each telling. A group of about 105 volunteer soldiers formed in Virginia City to march on the Indians.

The Virginia City war party finally encountered the Indians in a small valley located a few miles from Pyramid Lake. Ill-prepared for a battle, about two-thirds of the volunteers perished in the conflict.

The victory led to retaliation by regular army troops. At a second battle near Pyramid Lake, the outnumbered Indians were forced to scatter. To prevent further unrest, the U.S. Government decided to build Fort Churchill in July 1860.

The fort was also used to protect Pony Express riders, who would occasionally be harassed by Indians resentful of their passage through traditional Indian lands.

Later, the fort became one of the western outposts for the U.S. Army during the Civil War. While the Nevada garrison was never called into action during the war, it was an important training ground and supply depot for the Nevada Military District.

In 1869, the expense of maintaining the fort became too great for the U.S. Government, which decided to abandon the post and sell the buildings at an auction. At that time, most of the wooden roofs, supports and porches were removed and sold, but the adobe walls remained.

Much of the wood from the fort was used to build a two-story stagecoach stop, called Buckland's Station, that is still standing about a mile-and-a-half from the fort.

In 1957, following years of neglect and attempts to restore the buildings during the 1930s, the state of Nevada acquired Fort Churchill for the state park system. At that time, the state de-

Fort Churchill

cided to stabilize the ruins of the fort in what is called "preserved disrepair."

Today, visitors can often observe workers as they place new adobe bricks — manufactured from local clay — onto the worn walls. The bricks, which are authentic duplicates of the original materials used to build the fort, replace those that have been worn down by the elements.

At an excellent visitor center, which was built to resemble one of the original fort buildings, you can find a miniature replica of the fort as it appeared in the 1860s. Back then, the adobe walls were painted white and each building had a low-hanging shingled roof that also helped protect the walls.

Additionally, there are authentic U.S. Army uniforms and weapons from the fort on display, including a working cannon. A park ranger is available to answer any questions about the fort.

Across the road from the visitor center is the original cemetery. While the Army removed its dead when it abandoned the fort, you can still find the wooden markers for pioneer Nevadans from the area who were buried there.

Adjacent to the fort grounds in a pretty aspen grove along the banks of the Carson River is a developed camping and picnicking area. One of the best times of year to camp in the park is autumn when the aspens have turned vivid shades of yellow, brown and orange.

The Nevada Division of State Parks has 20 shaded campsites (with no hook ups), an RV dump station and picnic tables in the area. For more information, contact the Fort Churchill State Historic Monument, (702) 577-2345.

Fallon Museum Best Rural Repository

NEVADA IS BLESSED with a number of regional and local museums that are wonderful cache houses of the state's rich past. One of the best is the Churchill County Museum in Fallon.

Created in 1968, the 10,000 square foot museum is an impressive storehouse of artifacts detailing the development and history of Churchill County. It is a credit to the people of Fallon that the museum provides such a complete picture.

Historians have long known the Fallon area is an important nexus in man's development in the west. Before the arrival of settlers, native American people resided around the marshes and giant inland sea that once covered the area.

One of the best exhibits at the museum is a detailed display about Hidden Cave, an archaeological site with a 21,000-year stratigraphy (meaning that scientists can trace soil samples and fossils dating over that many years).

Free tours to Hidden Cave, located about 12 miles from Fallon, are offered through the museum on the second and fourth Saturday of each month at 9:30 a.m.

Additionally, the museum offers exhibits showing later area developments. There are good displays of Indian artifacts and one exhibit includes the remains of a covered wagon and other items used by settlers traveling on the Emigrant Trail through the nearby Forty Mile Desert (the most hazardous part of the trail).

Fallon is also located on the famed Pony Express Trail. The Overland Telegraph replaced the Pony Express riders and followed the same route. One exhibit describes the history of communication in the west and notes that the Overland Telegraph was eventually incorporated into the Churchill County Telephone and Telegraph System, the nation's only county-owned and maintained telephone system. (The museum sells souvenir glass telephone insulators that were once part of the system.)

The museum also contains a display telling the history of the Newlands Water Project, the first federal reclamation project in 1902. This irrigation system created the nearby Lahontan Reservoir and provides the water for area farmers.

Outside the museum building, you can also find a number of unique displays that further illustrate the area's history.

For example, there are samples of ancient Indian petroglyphs (rock writings) and the restored Woodliff Novelty Store, once a well-known Fallon business that served the local community over a century ago.

Reflecting the area's abundant agricultural roots, there is also a large collection of farming equipment, including a 1903 Case Steam Traction engine.

The museum has a small gift shop that offers one of the most complete collections of historic books about Nevada.

To reach the museum, drive east of Carson City for about an hour on Highway 50. Once in Fallon, turn right on Maine

Street. (It really should be called Main Street, but they like to do things a little differently in Fallon.) You'll find the museum at 1050 So. Maine St.

Of course, besides the museum, another reason to visit Fallon is to pick up some of the region's renowned produce. Fallon is the home of the Hearts of Gold cantaloupe, one of the juiciest and tastiest melons ever grown. Several local produce stores offer the Hearts of Gold in season (generally about late summer), including Workman's Produce on Highway 50.

Fallon celebrates its famous melons each year during the Cantaloupe Festival, held each Labor Day weekend.

While driving through Fallon, also take note of the Churchill County Courthouse, located at the intersection of Highway 50 and Maine Street. The building, constructed in 1903, is the only wooden courthouse still in use in the state.

The Churchill County Museum and Archives is open six days a week (closed Thursday). For more information, contact the museum at 1050 S. Maine St., Fallon, NV 89406, (702) 423-3677 or the Fallon Convention and Tourism Authority, 100 Campus Way, Fallon, NV 89406, (702) 423-4556.

Churchill County Museum

Grimes Point petroglyphs

Peak into Nevada's Past at Grimes Point, Hidden Cave

EVEN AFTER YEARS of study no one is quite sure how to interpret the centuries-old Indian "petroglyphs," or rock writings, that are found scratched on stone surfaces throughout the west, including Nevada.

Some of the best examples of these mysterious petroglyphs can be found at Grimes Point, about 12 miles east of Fallon on Highway 50.

Visitors to Grimes Point will find an interpretive trail that winds for about a mile through a small forest of engraved boulders and rocks. Petroglyphs in the area date more than 7,000 years old and contain a variety of styles, reflecting different eras.

A series of informative signs point out theories about the writings and the different types of symbols. For instance, the oldest petroglyphs are believed to be the simplest, a "pit and groove" pattern on several boulders. Later, the native Americans who scratched these designs carved more elaborate images, such as deer, lizards and the sun.

One sign notes that while some historians believe the writing has religious significance (representing a ritual asking the supreme being for a good hunt or harvest), other experts say they are simply prehistoric rock graffiti.

Regardless, there is something unique about wandering through the field of boulders and feeling you are in the presence of things that are very ancient.

Because of the relative isolation and remoteness, you walk on dusty trails surrounded by silence shattered only by the passing of an occasional car or truck and the sound of your own breathing. In the afternoon summer heat, it becomes easy to imagine someone sitting in the shade of one of the boulders and chipping a picture into the rock that represents the hot sun or the previous day's hunt.

About a mile north of Grimes Point is Hidden Cave, an archaeological dig site that offers a fascinating glimpse into the lifestyle of Nevada's original inhabitants.

Free tours of the cave are offered on the second and fourth Saturday of each month. Special tours are also available for groups of more than 12.

To take the tour, participants must meet at 9:30 a.m. at the Churchill County Museum at 1050 Maine Street in Fallon, then caravan to the cave for a tour, which lasts about two hours.

Discovered in the 1930s, Hidden Cave was excavated by archaeologists in 1940, then again in 1950 and from 1979-80. Following the latter explorations, the cave was stabilized as an interpretative exhibit.

The cave, which was utilized for thousands of years as a storage cache by migrating tribes, has been a veritable treasure trove for scientists, yielding a wide variety of prehistoric artifacts.

During several digs, archaeologists have found a considerable number of ancient nets, pots, tools, seeds and food remains. In fact, part of the reason the cave remained so undisturbed over the centuries is that it was for many years home for a large number of bats (who covered the inside of the cave with centuries of bat guano).

One of the most unique aspects of the cave is that it has been maintained as a dig site so that visitors can actually see how archaeologists study a site.

The walls are tagged with small markers indicating the various stratum or levels, which show age. For example, one layer is clearly white, showing that the cave floor was once covered with volcanic ash, which a guide explains was probably from an early eruption of Mount St. Helens.

The Churchill County Museum in Fallon, one of the finest small museums in the state, also has an excellent Hidden Cave exhibit that includes photographs of recent digs on the site.

For information about Grimes Point or Hidden Cave, contact the Bureau of Land Management, (702) 882-1631.

Sand Mountain

Sand Mountain is
Off-Roader's Dream

NOT MANY PEOPLE realize that much of Nevada was once underwater.

About 10,000 years ago, a giant inland sea, now known as Lake Lahontan, covered some 8,500 square miles including most of northern and central Nevada and parts of Oregon, Utah, California and Idaho.

The lake was formed from the melting of the great glaciers that once covered much of North America and has been described not as a solid body of water, but a series of long arms.

In the intervening years, the sea has receded (kind of like Jack Nicholson's hairline). All that remains are Pyramid and Walker lakes and a handful of dry lake beds such as the Humboldt and Carson sinks, the Black Rock Desert and Winnemucca Lake, near Pyramid Lake.

Another unique result of the disappearance of this sea was

the creation of Sand Mountain, located 32 miles east of Fallon on Highway 50 (about an hour-and-a-half from Carson City).

Sand Mountain was created when sand from surrounding flats, once part of the bottom of ancient Lake Lahontan, was blown against nearby mountain walls. Over centuries, the sand accumulated into a huge pile.

Today, visitors to Sand Mountain find a huge sand dune rising several hundred feet high — without an ocean.

The mountain is an off-road vehicle buff's dream. Any day, the massive sand mound is dotted with three and four-wheeled bikes, trikes and dune buggies skirting across the sandy surface.

In addition to hosting all those off-roaders, the mountain has been known to sing. Often at night, visitors can hear a whistling sound near the mountain. While rational people believe it occurs when wind skirts across the mountain surface, the rest of us know it is the mountain telling tales of stagecoaches, wagon trains and Pony Express riders who once passed by.

The mountain of sand isn't the only interesting thing about the area. Just a quarter-mile west of the turn-off to Sand Mountain is a dirt road leading to one of the best preserved Pony Express stations in Nevada. Be aware, however, the road is impassable during the winter months.

The ruins include several black stone walls that outline the site. About 20 years ago, the site was excavated by the University of Nevada, Reno and the Bureau of Land Management and is listed on the National Register of Historic Places.

Despite its relatively brief existence, the Pony Express continues to capture the imagination. The express only operated for 18 months, from April 3, 1860 to October 28, 1861. It ceased to operate four days after completion of the transcontinental telegraph system.

The route ran from St. Joseph, Mo., to Sacramento, Calif., and included 190 stations, 80 riders and 500 horses.

In Nevada, the Pony Express stretched 420 miles from the Antelope Valley (located about halfway between Ely and Wendover near the Utah border) to Lake Tahoe. Along the way were some 30 stations, of which only a few, like Sand Mountain (which was originally called the Sand Springs station) continue to exist.

The Sand Spring station is also notable because it was specifically mentioned in the diary of Sir Richard Burton, famed 19th century explorer and author.

Burton traveled with the Pony Express riders in the autumn of 1860. Of Sand Springs, he wrote "(It) deserves its name ... the land is cumbered here and there with drifted ridges of the finest sand, sometimes 200-feet high and shifting before every gale ... The station house was no unfit object in such a scene, roofless and chairless, filthy and squalid, with a smoky fire in one corner and a table in the centre of an impure floor, the walls open to every wind and interior full of dust."

For more information, contact the Bureau of Land Management, 882-5263.

Pony Express station

Pony Express Revisited

FOR EIGHTEEN MONTHS, a group of brave — some would say foolhardy — young men regularly rode more than 2,000 miles from St. Joseph, Missouri to Sacramento, California. Their job was to deliver mail and they were part of the Pony Express.

Despite the fact that it existed for such a short time, from April 3, 1860 to October 28, 1861, the fame of the Pony Express has endured. In fact, the National Park Service is exploring the possibility of designating the route as a national historic trail. Its demise was guaranteed four days before it closed by the completion of the first transcontinental telegraph wire.

In Nevada, the Pony Express route crossed the center of the state. The western half of the original route was roughly parallel to modern-day Highway 50 from Carson City to Austin. East of Austin, the route veers north of Highway 50 to the Ruby Marshes and into Utah.

Within Nevada, there were approximately 30 Pony Express stations (historians don't agree about the total number). Few of the stations were built for permanence, so little remains of most of the sites. However, explorers can find a few places that offer an intriguing glimpse into the difficult life of the Pony Express riders.

The stations were important to the riders because they were places to change horses, replenish supplies and pick up news before riding off to the next stop.

The western-most Nevada Pony Express station was a place called Friday's, located a mile east of Stateline at Lake Tahoe. The original blacksmith shop still stands, but is not open to the public because it sits on private land.

Just over the Sierra was the next stop, Genoa. The old post office in Genoa was used as the Pony Express station. The building has long since disappeared and today, the site is the vacant lot south of the courthouse.

From Genoa, the rider headed to Carson City. The original station is gone, but records show it was located on Carson Street between 4th and 5th streets.

The next stop was in Dayton, at a place called Spafford's Hall Station. That site is now a gravel pit (an historic marker just north of the downtown indicates the location) and a second Pony Express station was built on the site of the present Union Hotel.

From here, only a few of the remaining sites contain much to see, including three sites that offer the best ruins of the original stations.

One of those sites is Fort Churchill State Park, a Civil War-era fort that was built to defend Nevada settlers from hostile Indians. The fort also served as a visible reminder during the Civil War to the Confederacy that Nevada was part of the Union forces.

Further east is the Sand Springs Station, located south of massive Sand Mountain. Visitors here will find well preserved walls from the stone station that once provided a refuge to the riders (albeit an extremely dismal one). The site was excavated by University of Nevada, Reno, archaeologists and is listed on the National Register of Historic Places.

About 30 miles from Sand Mountain is the Cold Springs Station, which many consider the best preserved of the ruins. Located about a mile and half from Highway 50 (there is a wooden informational kiosk at the trailhead), the station has been studied by archaeologists and partially restored. It is also listed on the National Register.

We happen to know a bit about the Sand Springs and Cold Springs stations because both were included in a diary written in 1860 by British explorer Sir Richard Burton, who traveled the Pony Express route.

Of Sand Springs, Burton said, "The water near this vile hold was thick and stale with sulphury salts: it blistered even the hands."

Cold Springs was slightly more enticing, according to Burton, who described it as "a wretched place half built and wholly unroofed....Our animals, however, found good water in a rivulet from the neighboring hills."

The three best Pony Express stations to visit are: Fort Churchill, located 40 miles east of Carson City via Highway 50 and Alternate Highway 95; Sand Springs, located 25 miles east of Fallon, then a half-mile north of Highway 50; and Cold Springs, located 52 miles east of Fallon, then a mile-and-a-half hike south of the highway.

St. Augustine's Catholic Church, Austin

Visiting Austin like
Turning Back Clock

IF VIRGINIA CITY can rightly be called the "Silver Queen" because of the vast mineral wealth found there in the nineteenth century, then the mining town of Austin certainly deserves some claim to royalty — perhaps as the "Argenta Archduchess."

Austin's rich silver reserves were uncovered in 1862, a few years after the discovery of Virginia City's fabulous Comstock Lode. It was a heady time; every day seemed to bring word of some major gold or silver strike somewhere in Nevada.

By the end of the 1860s, Austin was Nevada's second largest city with more than 5,000 residents. The town had two newspapers, a railroad, a thriving downtown district, a national bank branch and the foundations for three churches.

Like every other Nevada mining town, however, when the ore began to disappear, the people soon followed. Although more than $50 million in silver was produced in Austin, by the 1890s the town had begun its slide from an active mining town to a sleepy road town dependent on passing traffic.

Austin, which is located about 170 miles east of Carson City on U.S. Highway 50, has avoided the fate of most mining towns — namely becoming a ghost town — and is today one of the better examples of the kind of 19th century mining towns that once dotted the Nevada landscape.

A visit to Austin is an opportunity to turn back the clock. This is a place filled with character. You can feel something different about this town when you walk the main street or climb the steep hills to explore back alleys.

Sure, the buildings are leaning a bit, the sidewalks aren't level and brickwork on some walls seems a tad unstable — but that's all part of Austin's charm.

It is obvious that Austin has seen better days. The town's bank closed several years ago. (It has been replaced by a credit union.) More populous Battle Mountain to the north took away the county seat some time back, and the town's newspaper, which claims to be the oldest continually published newspaper in the state, is actually printed in Tonopah.

But most importantly, Austin has survived. Mining continues to bring in new money and the road traffic is fairly steady with tourists traveling across Highway 50 through the scenic beauty of central Nevada.

Austin is worth the trip. The town is filled with unique historic buildings, such as Stokes Castle on the southwest end of town. As you drive into Austin from the west, you can't help but notice this strange stone tower on the hillside overlooking the nearby Reese River Valley.

Stokes Castle was built in 1897 by Anson Phelps Stokes to resemble a Roman tower. Stokes, who owned considerable mining interests in the area and constructed the 92-mile Nevada Central Railroad line from Battle Mountain to Austin, built the three-story tower as a summer home. The tower was only used for a few years, but has remained an interesting architectural oddity.

Austin is also notable for having three magnificent frontier churches. The oldest is St. Augustine's Catholic Church, built in 1866. While no longer used for regular services, local residents have restored portions of the impressive red brick building and hope to reestablish a parish in Austin.

The Methodist Church, also built in 1866, was once the finest church in the state. The structure was financed from mining stock donated to the church, and has since been converted into a community center.

St. George's Episcopal Church, built in 1878, is the only one of the town's historic houses of worship that remains in use. This particularly lovely church was actually financed by a single pass of a collection plate on Easter 1877.

Just west of the main portion of downtown Austin is the restored Gridley Store, built in the early 1860s from native stone. Reuel Gridley, owner of the store, gained considerable fame about 125 years ago after he lost an election bet and agreed to carry a 50-pound sack of flour the length of the town.

Following his trek, the sack of flour was returned to the center of town where it was auctioned, with the proceeds going to the "Sanitary Fund" (predecessor to today's Red Cross). The sack was sold many times that day, each buyer returning it to be auctioned again, raising more than $6,000 for the fund.

Other communities heard about Gridley's famous sack of flour and he was invited to conduct similar auctions throughout the west. Over the course of the next year, Gridley actually raised about $275,000 for the fund, which largely aided Civil War victims. The sack is on display at the Nevada Historical Society in Reno.

In addition to history, Austin also offers plenty of outdoor recreational opportunities. Because it is located in the Toiyabe

Range, visitors will find a number of good hiking and camping spots, including the Bob Scott Campground, just east of town, and Kingston Canyon, located 35 miles southeast of Austin via State Route 376.

For more information, contact the Greater Austin Chamber of Commerce, Court House, Box 212, Austin, NV 89310, (702) 964-2200.

The Loneliest Town on
the Loneliest Road

THE PEOPLE OF EUREKA are so proud of their relative isolation that they've taken to calling their community the "loneliest town on the loneliest road."

Fortunately, that doesn't mean there isn't anything to do in this historic community. In fact, while it's located in the center of Nevada about 240 miles from Reno, Eureka is one of the most picturesque of the state's 19th century mining towns.

Silver and lead were discovered in the Eureka area in 1864, but it wasn't until 1869 that smelters were constructed that helped make extracting the ore feasible.

Eureka produced far more mineral wealth than did neighboring Austin — but never developed the hell-raising image of its sister city. By 1878, Eureka had a population of 8,000 and had surpassed Austin as the second largest city in Nevada.

It was during that period that Eureka began constructing a

number of large brick buildings — and fortunately for us, many are still standing — including the Eureka Courthouse (1879), the Eureka Sentinel offices (1879), the Eureka Theatre (1879) and the Jackson House (1877).

Part of the reason for the sturdy construction, which was somewhat unusual in a 19th century mining town, was a disastrous fire, in April 1879, that destroyed most of the wooden buildings. When the town was rebuilt, it used brick and fireproof iron shutters and doors.

In 1875, Eureka was connected to the world by the Eureka and Palisade Railroad, which ran north to a depot in Carlin. While the tracks and equipment were sold when the railroad ceased operations in 1937, it is still possible to see the rail bed alongside State Route 278, the road that stretches from Eureka to Carlin.

As probably Nevada's best preserved mining town, Eureka is a great place to explore. An informative, historic walking brochure is available from the Eureka Chamber of Commerce or from the *Eureka Sentinel* Museum, which is open during the summer months.

The *Sentinel* building has been converted into a fine small museum. The museum displays the old *Sentinel* newspaper equipment as well as other exhibits detailing the history of this fascinating town.

The two-story red brick courthouse on Main Street towers over the community. Over the years, the courthouse has been maintained and restored, making it one of the best preserved examples of late 19th century architecture in the state.

Across the street are the Jackson House and the Eureka Theatre. The former has been converted into a restaurant and rooming house while the latter is awaiting restoration by the county, which recently acquired it for a community center.

A special treat is a visit with Frank and Carol Bleuss, owners of the Parsonage House bed and breakfast. Frank Bleuss is a master carpenter who built the B&B from a 19th century miner's shack.

Little of the original structure remains, but Bleuss has built a marvel of incredible wood paneling and handcrafted furniture (some with secret compartments). Guests will also find a well-stocked wine cellar and modern kitchen.

The Bleuss' home is also intriguing; they live in a restored 1870s church located adjacent to the Parsonage House.

The walking brochure also describes other buildings throughout the town. For more information, contact the Eureka Chamber of Commerce, Box 14, Eureka, NV 89316.

Eureka Theatre, Eureka

Nevada Northern Railway, Ely

Rolling on the Nevada Northern Railway Museum

THE NEVADA NORTHERN Railway Museum in eastern Nevada offers a unique opportunity to visit a working railroad that some historians have called the "best preserved shortline railroad in America."

Nearly everything, from oak roll-top desks to the dirt floor blacksmith shop, is the way it was during the 80 years that the Nevada Northern provided regular service in the Ely, Nevada area.

"When you go into the museum, it looks like on a Friday afternoon, everybody just got and up, went home for the weekend and never returned," said museum director Lorraine Ulibarri, "which is just about how it happened when the railroad shut down."

Ulibarri said that the oak desks, filing cabinets and even the black ceramic telephones in the depot building are original equipment, installed when the railroad was built in 1906 by the Nevada Consolidated Copper Company, which later became part of the Kennecott Copper Company. She said that the railroad, which ceased operating in 1983, never replaced or removed anything.

Ulibarri said, "It's amazing what's still there. They have complete records of the cost of every piece of rail that was ever purchased."

And best of all, Ulibarri said, "Visitors can ride on the Nevada Northern Railway." An hour-and-a-half trip on the old steam engine #40 travels from the East Ely depot to "Keystone," to the nearby copper mines — or you can take a vintage Alco diesel train along the "Hiline" route through the beautiful Steptoe Valley. Trains operate every weekend May 18 through October 20, and on selected Wednesday's during the season.

The Nevada Northern Railway Museum is located in Ely, Nevada, a quiet, charming community of about 6,000 residents that serves as a center for business and commerce in eastern Nevada.

Guided tours of the museum begin with a walk through the two-story East Ely Depot building, the centerpiece of the museum. Inside, visitors will find elegant, antique wood and brass ticket windows, benches and light fixtures.

At the Transportation Building, several Nevada Northern locomotives are on display, including a rare, 1907 steam-powered rotary snow plow, a massive steam-powered crane, also built in 1907, and a handsome, steam ten-wheel Baldwin locomotive, old Number 40, built in 1910.

Other buildings house many of the 60 pieces of rolling stock owned by the museum, including early 20th century ore cars, flat cars, cabooses and a 1917 coach car that was converted into a rolling bunk house for workers.

A gift shop, the Rail Place, offers a selection of railroad memorabilia, books and other items.

The Nevada Northern was built in 1905-06 by the Nevada

Consolidated Copper Company to haul copper ore from mines at Copper Flat, located west of Ely, to a smelter in McGill, about 9 miles north of Ely.

After processing, the copper was transported from McGill to the Southern Pacific Railroad lines at Cobre, about 130 miles to the north.

By 1908, passenger service was offered on the line. Eventually, more than four million passengers would travel on the Nevada Northern Railway. A special daily school train carried McGill youngsters to Ely until 1941.

In 1915, Kennecott Copper Company began acquiring the stock of the Nevada Consolidated Copper Company, completing the transaction in 1932. The railroad continued operations until 1983, when Kennecott decided to shut down the copper mines, the smelter and the railroad, which were no longer financially practical.

By 1985, Kennecott donated to the city of Ely the East Ely Depot, the adjacent buildings, several miles of track and the railroad rolling stock.

For more information, contact the Nevada Northern Railway Museum, P.O. Box 40, East Ely, NV 89315, (702) 289-2085.

Stella Lake, Great Basin National Park

Nevada's Great Basin National Park is Untouched Wonderland

A BRISK WIND shakes the few needles growing on the twisted, groping limb of the centuries-old Bristlecone Pine tree. Ahead, the bright sun reflects off glacial ice at the base of Wheeler Peak. Way up here, it's hard to imagine that only minutes away are miles of flat hot desert and sagebrush.

Eastern Nevada's new Great Basin National Park represents well the amazing contrasts found in the west's unique Great Basin terrain.

The park boasts an exceptionally wide range of plant and animal habitats extending from the Upper Sonoran Life Zone, characterized by jack rabbits, sagebrush and cacti, to the frigid Arctic Alpine Tundra Life Zone at the higher elevations.

The 77,109-acre park, located about 70 miles east of Ely, Nev., on U.S. Highway 50 and State Route 487, is America's newest national park in more than a decade.

The area was selected for national park designation in 1986 and includes stunning mountain peaks, lush meadows, fascinating limestone caves and scenic overlooks. Surrounded by wide desert valleys, the park has been described as a luxurious island in the sky.

The Great Basin National Park is only America's 49th national park. While relatively small compared to some parks, like Yellowstone, it is roughly the same size as Arches National Park and twice as big as Bryce Canyon National Park, both in nearby Utah.

The park is located in the Snake Mountain Range, an impressive wall of rock that rises spectacularly above the surrounding valleys.

Like all of Nevada's mountains — and Nevada is the most mountainous state with more than 150 ranges — the Snake Range runs north to south in a curious pattern that one geologist has described as resembling caterpillars marching toward Mexico.

The Snake Range is dissected into two parts by Highway 50. The upper range contains 12,067-foot Mount Moriah. To the south, in the lower range, Wheeler Peak is the tallest point at 13,063-feet. and the heart of the new Great Basin National Park.

The entrance to the new park is located on the eastern face of the range, just beyond the tiny community of Baker. There you can find some services, including a small motel, restaurants and a gas station.

The Visitors Center, located about five miles west of Baker on State Route 74, is also the gateway to Lehman Caves, a fascinating wonderland of limestone formations. Additionally, there is also a small gift shop, restaurant and informative displays.

The caves were discovered in 1885 by a local farmer named Absalom S. Lehman. Lehman had tried his hand at mining in California and Australia, with limited success, before settling in eastern Nevada to grow food for nearby mining camps.

One day, he stumbled upon a gaping hole in the mountainside above his ranch. Curious about his discovery, he climbed inside with a candle lantern and found a fabulous series of underground chambers. The caves were declared a National Monument in 1922 and have continued to intrigue visitors over the years.

In the early days, visitors crawled through some of the passageways, but today, a 90-minute guided tour covers about six-tenths of a mile on developed paths and stairs. Because you are deep in the ground, visitors are cautioned to dress warmly.

The caves were carved out of the surrounding limestone millions of years ago by underground streams. The unique formations were created by carbon-dioxide-charged water gradually filtering through cracks in the limestone. The water dissolved the limestone, then slowly reformed into the fascinating rock sculptures you see.

Visitors find stalagmites hanging from the ceilings like massive teeth and imposing stalagmites rising from the floors. Occasionally, the two merge into huge pillars that almost seem to support the ceiling.

The caves are notable because of the large variety of formations, such as twisting helictites, bubbly cave coral and the unique circular shields or palettes.

North of the Visitors Center is a 12-mile road to the base of Wheeler Peak. The drive offers a spectacular view of the peak and Snake Valley.

Three campgrounds are located along the scenic drive. The Wheeler Peak Campground at 10,000-feet offers 37 sites, the Upper Lehman Creek Campground has 24 spaces and the Lower Lehman Campground has 11 spaces.

At Wheeler Campground, there is also a trailhead for several trails that lead to various lakes, groves of Bristlecone Pine trees, the glacier and Wheeler Peak. Maps of major trails and lakes are available at the Visitors Center.

Additional undeveloped campsites are located south of the Visitors Center at Baker Creek. A trailhead near the Baker Creek sites is the start of 7 miles of marked trails leading to Baker Lake, Jefferson Peak and Washington Peak.

The ancient Bristlecones are one of the featured attractions at the park. Like the face of an old cowboy, these gnarled, twisted trees possess the character and dignity that comes from having taken life's best shots and survived. The park contains some of the oldest examples of these trees, which can live for more than 4,000 years.

Lexington Arch, located near the southeast border of the park, is a natural limestone arch more than six stories high. An unpaved road leads to a trailhead from which you can hike two miles to the picturesque arch.

About 70 miles east of the park is Ely, a full-service community with hotels, motels, restaurants, grocery stores, gas stations and RV parking.

For more information, contact the Great Basin National Park, Baker, NV 89311, (702) 234-7331 or the White Pine Chamber of Commerce, 636 Aultman, Ely, NV 89301, (702) 289-8877.

PART V

The Humboldt Trail

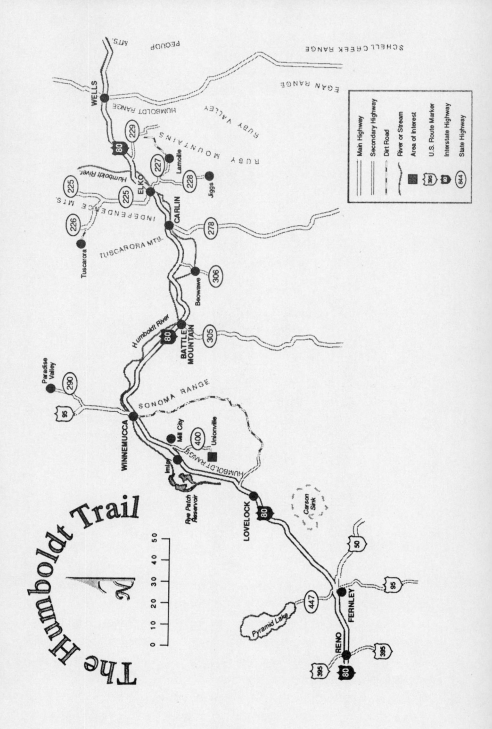

The Humboldt Trail

One of the pleasantest and most invigorating exercises one can contrive is to run and jump across the Humboldt River till he is overheated, and then drink it dry.

— Mark Twain, *Roughing It*

THE HUMBOLDT TRAIL was the main route across Nevada for frontier travelers heading toward the promised land of California. It was a difficult and hazardous journey through a harsh and un-friendly land.

The trail roughly paralleled the Humboldt River, which, according to some estimates, is so windy with switchbacks and loops that it would actually be four times longer than it is if it was stretched out in a straight line.

The Humboldt River, as noted by Twain, is also a body of water prone to great fluctuations in flow. In a normal year, it practically dries up in most parts during the late summer, but has been known to cause flooding in Elko and Winnemucca in the spring during wet years.

As a part of the famous Emigrant Trail, the Humboldt Trail is a route rich with history. The route was originally traveled by the west's earliest non-native American explorers, such as Peter Skene Ogden, who trapped along the Humboldt in 1829.

In 1843, John C. Fremont led an expedition along the Humboldt while searching for the northwest passage, a water route that would connect the Atlantic and Pacific oceans. Fremont, in fact, is responsible for mapping much of the route and providing names to many of the landmarks.

Later, in 1844, the first wagon trains began to rumble across Nevada, following the Humboldt, before crossing the infamous 40-mile Desert, a stretch of barren dry land between the end of the Humboldt River, at the Humboldt Sink near Lovelock, and the Carson River.

Over the next quarter century, until the Central Pacific Railroad line was completed in 1869, the Humboldt Trail was a veritable pioneer highway across the vast expanses of Nevada. Traffic accelerated after the discovery of gold in California in 1849.

Today, the Humboldt Trail has become part of Interstate 80, a modern, four-lane asphalt track that spans the U.S. Where once wagons and oxen slowly trudged over a muddy trail through the sagebrush, there are now giant diesel trucks and hundreds of shiny air-conditioned automobiles racing across the state.

Many of the towns along the way trace their roots to the Emigrant Trail, starting out as trading posts or watering holes. Later, with the coming of the railroad, other towns appeared to serve as depots, switching stations and maintenance facilities.

The pieces in this section only scratch the surface of the history and color of this fascinating part of Nevada. Whether you call it the Humboldt Trail, the Emigrant Trail, the Central Pacific Railroad line or Interstate 80, it is clear that the route has always played an important role in the transportation systems that helped develop and sustain the American West.

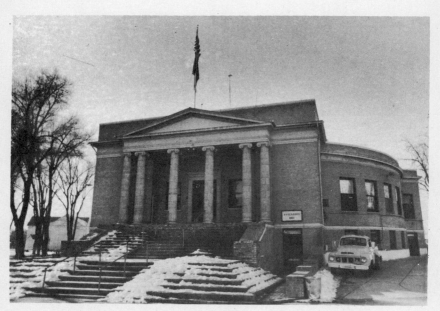

"Round" Courthouse, Lovelock

Lovelock in the Heart
of the State

LOVELOCK HAS ALWAYS held an important place in the development of Nevada and the American West.

The west's earliest explorers, Peter Skene Ogden, Kit Carson and John C. Fremont, passed through the region, stopped to take note of the area's grassy plains and plentiful ground water. They called it Big Meadows.

Later, immigrants to California followed the Humboldt River across Nevada, then stopped at the Big Meadows to refresh their cattle and restock their supplies of water and hay before embarking across the dreaded Forty Mile Desert.

In fact, Lovelock continues to serve an important role as a stop for travelers needing a quiet moment or some refreshments while traveling Interstate 80.

In the 1860s and 1870s, the area became an important mining center, with major gold and silver strikes at nearby

Unionville, Oreana and Rochester. In fact, Unionville was one of young Sam Clemens' first homes in Nevada — before he abandoned the tough life of gold miner for a career as a newspaperman in Virginia City.

The area gained its present identity in 1866, when Englishman George Lovelock purchased land there and donated 80 acres to the Central Pacific Railroad for a townsite that was called "Lovelock's." The name was shortened in 1922.

As mining dwindled, agriculture and ranching became more important. At the turn of the century, Lovelock was the location of the ranch of John G. Taylor, owner of one of the west's great cattle empires. At one time, Taylor owned 60,000 head of sheep, 8,000 cattle, 130,000 acres of land and leased another half-million acres.

Additionally, the meadows proved ideal for growing crops such as barley, wheat, oats and alfalfa. The latter continues to be one of the region's main crops.

Today, Lovelock, located 90 miles east of Reno on Interstate 80, is a friendly, small, Nevada agricultural community.

It boasts a number of interesting buildings, including the Pershing County Courthouse, the only round hall of justice in use in America. (There's an old joke about the courthouse: "My wife and I were divorced in Lovelock — and we're still going around in circles.")

Visitors will also find picnic tables and a playground in the quiet, shaded areas around the round courthouse.

Downtown Lovelock has other good examples of typical frontier development, including a classic train depot building and several residences. Local residents are attempting to raise money to save the railroad building.

One of the best places to learn more about the development of the Lovelock area is the Marzen House Museum, just west of the downtown on old U.S. 40. The museum is located in one of the community's oldest and most impressive homes, a two-story ranch house built more than a century ago.

Lovelock is also an important archaeological site. The nearby Lovelock Cave, which is not open to the public, was first excavated in 1924 and was one of the west's first major archaeological digs, yielding important native American artifacts.

Additionally, the landscape about 20 miles west of Lovelock is covered with intriguing tufa (pronounced too-fah) rock formations. Tufa is created when calcium-filled springs gurgle up through salty (carbonate) water. The chemical bonding of the two results in the limestonelike substance called tufa.

The area outside of Lovelock was once covered by a receding salten sea. Alkali flats south of the interstate are remains of this giant inland ocean.

The Lovelock area rocks were formed over years as the calcium material collected around springs. The reaction only occurs in the lake itself. When the water recedes and exposes the tufa formations, they stop growing.

For more information, contact the Lovelock-Pershing County Chamber of Commerce, P.O. Box 821, Lovelock, NV 89419, or call (702) 273-7213.

Unionville

Mark Twain's Unionville

BEFORE HE BEGAN writing under the name, "Mark Twain," for Virginia City's *Territorial Enterprise* newspaper, young Sam Clemens made a visit to the mining camp of Unionville to try his hand at prospecting.

Clemens arrived in the town during the winter of 1861 and staked several claims. After a few days of actual digging (all of about 12 feet) and mucking, however, Clemens decided there had to be an easier way to make a living.

He tried, unsuccessfully, to play the local mining stock market before departing for Virginia City and his ultimate fame.

Located about half-way between Lovelock and Winnemucca, Unionville offers a glimpse into Nevada's mining past. To reach it, travel east of Lovelock on Interstate 80 to the Mill City exit. Head south on State Route 400 for about 15 miles, then drive west for three miles on a good dirt road.

Despite Clemens' less than profitable experiences in Unionville, the area did have a handful of mines that produced good quality ore. A party of prospectors were led to the area in early 1861 by a band of Paiutes who discovered rich silver ore in the Buena Vista Canyon.

By July, a mining district had been created and a small town was beginning to develop at the mouth of the canyon By 1863, nearly 800 people lived in the area, which was named⸱ the first Humboldt County seat. The town also boasted a newspaper, a horse-drawn trolley line, a town hall and a school house.

The prosperity was short-lived. While the mines continued to produce well into the 1870s, Winnemucca eclipsed Unionville as the center of commerce in the county because of its location as a railroad stop. Eventually the county seat was moved to Winnemucca, as did many of Unionville's businesses and people.

Fortunately for us, Unionville has never been entirely abandoned. Today's visitors will find an assortment of ruins amidst a handful of residences. The picturesque old school house remains (although it is not open to the public).

There are no services in Unionville, but the community does have one of the most peaceful and quaint bed and breakfast inns in Nevada, the Old Pioneer Garden.

The Pioneer Garden is part old Unionville and part new. Owners Harold and Mitzi Jones began with two original Unionville stone walls and built their inn around them.

The result is a homey two-story building (which was originally a wagon maker's home) with six bedrooms and four baths. Because of its relative isolation, Unionville is a perfect place for someone looking for a quiet retreat. The Joneses have filled the inn with rustic country furnishings, including an antique iron stove used for heating in the winter.

For visitors desiring a little more privacy, there is also a two-bedroom cabin adjacent to the main house.

As befits a good bed and breakfast, the morning meals are memorable. Guests generally are treated to a number of dishes including buttermilk pancakes made with homeground corn meal and stuffed with fresh fruit. The Joneses also allow use of their large kitchen for other meals.

One of the amazing things about Unionville is that it seems like it shouldn't be there. The road to the town stretches through an extremely dry valley bordered by brown hills.

But when you head up into Buena Vista Canyon, you suddenly enter a kind of oasis. A creek runs through the community and nourishes a beltway of trees and thick vegetation (as well as some pretty good brown trout, according to locals).

You will find a pleasant hike along the creek up through the canyon. Adjacent to the stream is a dirt road that eventually leads to Lovelock. The condition of the road, however, makes it only advisable for those with four-wheel drive or off-road vehicles.

The mountainsides above Unionville are covered with the tailing piles and remains of the community's once-thriving mines. You might even find all of Sam Clemens' 12-foot shaft, if you look real hard.

For more information, contact the Old Pioneer Garden, (702) 538-7585.

Nixon Opera House, Winnemucca

Paved Streets — But
no Sea Lions

FOR THE PAST FEW YEARS, the city of Winnemucca has dared to be funny.

While conventional wisdom says communities should promote themselves with exciting or enticing slogans, the town of Winnemucca has capitalized on its unusual name with a handful of clever, self-deprecating slogans.

Like the old Burma Shave signs, Winnemucca looked to billboards to carry its message. The signs, which were placed along Interstate 80 between Salt Lake City and Reno, had simple phrases such as: "Winnemucca — City of Paved Streets," "Winnemucca — No Caves, No Sea Lions" and "What's a Winnemucca?"

Maybe it was because of the town's funny-sounding name, but the campaign has worked, providing travelers on the interstate with an absolutely irresistible reason for stopping there — who could pass up a town that was obviously having so much fun?

Ironically, there are more than a few things notable in Winnemucca. Its name is derived from a great Paiute leader, Chief Winnemucca, who, despite his involvement in the Pyramid Lake War of 1860 (Nevada's only true battle fought in anger), attempted to maintain peace between his people and the growing population of white settlers.

The Chief's daughter, Sarah Winnemucca, was the first Indian woman to publish a book in English and was a respected teacher, interpreter and lecturer in the late 19th century.

Winnemucca has long been an important crossroads in the development of Nevada and the American West. In the 1830s, the earliest explorers camped in the area while following the Humboldt River. Later, it became a trading post for wagon trains traveling through Nevada on the journey to California.

In the 1880s, the transcontinental railroad was built through Winnemucca, which became an important shipping point.

In 1900, Winnemucca was the site of a spectacular bank robbery reportedly committed by the notorious Butch Cassidy and the Hole in the Wall Gang.

Unfortunately for the romantics in Winnemucca, historians have disputed the story, agreeing the bank was robbed, and speculating that Hole in the Wall Gang members may have participated, but doubting that Butch or the Sundance Kid ever set foot in the town.

Today, Winnemucca is a friendly, growing community in the shadow of the beautiful Santa Rosa mountain range. The town is located 180 miles east of Reno via Interstate 80.

One of the most prominent buildings in town is Nixon Hall on Winnemucca Boulevard. Built in 1907 as an opera house, it was later donated to the city by banker George Nixon (the same bank allegedly robbed by Butch and the boys), who left Winnemucca to become a U.S. Senator.

The 500-room theater has a classic art deco design. Winnemuccans are attempting to raise money to restore the impressive building.

Adjacent to Nixon Hall are the Winnemucca Chamber of Commerce offices and the Buckaroo Hall of Fame, both located inside a former casino building. The Hall of Fame is a fine small collection of local and regional cowboy history, arts and crafts, including saddles, spurs, hand-crafted ropes and rare photographs. The hall is open daily from 8 a.m. to 5 p.m.

Perhaps the best thing about visiting Winnemucca is eating at one of its fine Basque restaurants. The town boasts three, including the venerable Winnemucca Hotel, built in 1863, Ormachea's Dinner House and the excellent Martin Hotel, located adjacent to the railroad tracks.

Across the Humboldt River from the main part of Winnemucca is the Humboldt Museum. The museum complex includes the restored century-old St. Mary's Episcopal Church and a newer brick structure beside the church.

Inside, visitors will find a collection of exhibits that tell the story of the area, including an antique automobile collection and native American artifacts.

Like many Nevada towns, Winnemucca hosts a variety of special events. Among the most interesting are: the Western Art Roundup on Labor Day weekend, a major regional western art show; the Mule Race and Show in June; the Winnemucca Basque Festival in mid-June; and the Winnemucca Rodeo, one of the oldest in the state.

Just north of Winnemucca is the Santa Rosa range, one of the most beautiful and least known wilderness areas in the state. The range offers good hiking trails and a wonderful, pristine landscape.

Sixteen miles east of Winnemucca on the interstate is the former mining town of Golconda. At the turn of the century,

Golconda achieved regional fame for its hot springs hotels.

About a half-dozen resorts grew up in the area although none have survived various fires and economic downturns that plagued the community over the past century. Other than a few saloons, some weathered houses and a school house, not much remains of Golconda.

Forty miles north of Winnemucca, nestled on the east side of the Santa Rosas, is Paradise Valley, a quiet agricultural valley with a handful of extremely photogenic historic buildings.

An hour north of Winnemucca is McDermitt, on the Oregon border. This tiny village includes the Fort McDermitt Reservation, home of the colorful Red Mountain Pow Wow in June.

Nearby is the Virgin Valley, location of the highly-prized black fire opals. For a fee, visitors can hunt for the precious stones on a handful of local gemfields.

For more information, contact the Winnemucca Chamber of Commerce, 46 Winnemucca Boulevard, Winnemucca, NV 89445, or call (702) 623-2225.

Paradise Valley:
Hidden Oasis of the
Santa Rosa Range

THE SKY OVERHEAD was painted a beautiful shade of pale blue. A weathered, gray, wooden two-story building was framed by large cottonwoods. It was all picture perfect.

Paradise Valley is one of Nevada's loveliest and most enchanting places. Set in the shadows of the Santa Rosa mountain range, the valley is an unexpected treat for those traveling north of Winnemucca.

To reach Paradise Valley, travel 22 miles northeast of the central Nevada community of Winnemucca on Nevada State Route 290.

Founded in 1864, the Paradise Valley has always been noted for its rich and fertile soil. While there has been some mining in the surrounding mountains, from the start, Paradise Valley has been a ranching and farming community.

The vast grassy fields that encircle the tiny hamlet are dotted with fat cattle. Walking the well-shaded roads, it's difficult not to be overwhelmed by the peacefulness. Traffic is virtually nonexistent and people go on with their business.

A cowboy rides across a golden field just west of town. Sitting tall and erect in his worn leather saddle, he slowly circled around a group of cows, gently prompting them to continue strolling toward a gate.

Down the street is an old, white Victorian-style house that conjures up images of Edna Purviance, a silent movie star who was born and raised in this valley. Perhaps she lived in that house for a time, or attended a classmate's birthday party there.

Purviance, who is largely forgotten in Nevada, later moved to Lovelock, then on to San Francisco where she was discovered by Charlie Chaplin. She appeared in nearly 40 films with Chaplin before calling it quits.

Not really a ghost town because it has an active post office, Odd Fellows Hall, saloon, grocery store and gas pump, Paradise Valley has the same kind of feel of antiquity found in Nevada ghost towns.

Visitors will find plenty of abandoned historic buildings and ruins dating back to the town's earliest days.

At the north end of the village are the most picturesque structures. There is an intriguing two-story saloon — with a name that time and the elements have made hard to decipher.

Adjacent is a brown brick building with a sagging, white wooden balcony. Inside, two cats growl, then make parrying sounds. One can imagine the two of them circling like wary boxers, each searching for a weakness in the other's defenses.

Across the street — and not one car passing during a recent hour-long walk through the town — there are a few aging, white-washed wooden houses and a beautiful old brown-red barn that overlooks a creek running through the town. At the end of the block is the remains of a general store that once had a gas pump.

The road through Paradise Valley continues to Hinckey Summit (elevation 7,867 feet), which affords a spectacular view of the valley and is the easiest way into the Santa Rosa range.

The road becomes gravel just a few miles beyond the town of Paradise Valley (it should only be driven during dry months) and leads into the mountain range, which recently gained national wilderness designation.

The Santa Rosas are one of the state's least-known mountain areas. Rising to more than 9,700-feet (Granite Peak), the mountains are largely undeveloped and underutilized. Hikers will find several alpine lakes and some gorgeous, untouched mountain scenery in the range.

The road passes through the heart of the range, offering a memorable scenic drive through this rugged wilderness country. About 40 miles north of the town of Paradise Valley, the road drops out of the mountains and connects with U.S. Highway 95.

North is the McDermitt Indian Reservation, home of the Red Mountain Indian Powwow in September, and the small community of McDermitt straddling the Nevada-Oregon border. McDermitt is home of one of the state's oldest amateur rodeos.

For more information, contact the Winnemucca Chamber of Commerce, 46 Winnemucca Boulevard, Winnemucca, NV 89445, or call (702) 623-2225.

Paradise Valley

Northeastern Nevada Museum, Elko

Buckaroo Life Celebrated
in America's Last
True Cowtown

WRITER LOWELL THOMAS once called Elko the last true cowtown in America.

And as home of the world famous Cowboy Poetry Gathering, the J. M. Capriola Western Shop and the C. S. Garcia Saddle Shop, it's easy to see why someone would say that about Elko.

Elko is the real west, not the reel west found in the movies. The cowboys you find out here are the genuine article, with dirt, sweat and the pungent smell of sagebrush on their clothing.

Most of the time, however, the only places you'll see these guys is on the range or working one of the large spreads outside of Elko. Occasionally a few amble into town to raise some hell or have a worn pair of boots repaired.

But the absolute best place to find a real buckaroo is at the Cowboy Poetry Gathering, held the last weekend of January at the Elko Convention Center.

Started six years ago, the gathering has grown from an informal get-together for a few dozen cowboys to an international event that, in recent years, has attracted thousands.

Strange as it sounds, cowboys have long had a tradition of reciting poetry. Generally, these poems — really stories in rhyme — were shared when cowboys would sit around a campfire after a hard day on the range.

As with cowboy music, cowboy poetry developed as. a result of the long hours that cowboys spent alone on the range. To pass the time, many would concoct songs and poems about the things they saw or experienced — and, in some cases, exaggerate those episodes.

The gathering was created when western folklife expert Hal Cannon heard about buckaroos in various places throughout the west who recited poetry. Cannon decided to see how widespread was this unique western art form..

He helped organize the first gathering in 1985 and found it was not only a popular form of expression for cowboys, but extremely entertaining for the public. Since then, attendance has grown from 600 to more than 7,000 people.

The event consists of a series of poetry and music workshops during the day, followed by evening performances featuring the best and most unique poets and musicians. There are also usually displays of cowboy arts, such as saddle-making, and photography exhibits.

The workshops, which are free, are organized around a theme, such as "Nevada Cowboy Poets," "Traditional Music" or "Cowboy Humor." During the sessions, participating cowboys, who are all working buckaroos, recite poetry and often explain the development of the work.

The evening performances, which are often sold out months in advance, often feature more well-known poets, such as Baxter Black, Waddie Mitchell and Don Edwards, as well as notable musicians. In recent years, performers have included Michael Martin Murphey, Jerry Jeff Walker and Rambling Jack Elliott — and you frequently don't know what surprise guest is going to show up and pick a few tunes.

For those interested in purchasing cowboy items, Elko's western shops are legendary. The Caprioli store is a local institution filled with everything the want-to-be buckaroo could need.

The Garcia saddle shop, located upstairs from Caprioli's, is renowned for the quality of its hand-crafted saddles. Customers have included Will Rogers, Bing Crosby and Sylvester Stallone.

Not everything in Elko is cowboy. Located about 300 miles east of Reno via Interstate 80, the community is in the heart of Nevada's active gold mining country. Nearby Carlin is the site of the world's largest gold mine.

Elko also boasts a significant Basque population. Basque people came to Nevada at the turn of the century to work as sheepherders in the wide open ranges of Nevada.

As a result of the Basque presence, Elko has several fine Basque restaurants, including the Star Hotel (located in an atmospheric old wooden two-story boarding house), Biltoki (a Basque word meaning "the gathering place") and the Nevada Dinner House.

At the Star, meals are served family-style, with patrons sitting side-by-side at long tables draped with red and white checked tablecloths. Diners find plenty of food — at traditional Basque restaurants, such as the Star, food is served until you're satiated.

At all three, meals often include authentic Basque fare, such as sweetbreads, tongue and "bacalao" (a salty fish dish) as well as more standard dishes, such as marinated beef steak and lamb.

To celebrate the region's Basque heritage, the town is home of the National Basque Festival, held on the July 4th weekend. The annual event attracts Basques from throughout the west as well as those who enjoy three days of dancing, eating and watching competitions between Basque strongmen, sheepherders and dancers.

The festival begins with a parade and is followed by a day of contests that can include chopping wood, rounding up sheep and lifting and dragging huge concrete cylinders and stones. In the evening, everyone sits down to a Basque barbecue featuring sausages, beans, marinated lamb and other delectable treats.

Elko also claims one of the best small museums in Nevada with its Northeastern Nevada Museum. There, you will find quality displays on the cowboy lifestyle, Basques, the Emigrant Trail (which passed through Elko) and wildlife indigenous to the area.

The region around Elko includes many of Nevada's most beautiful mountain scenic areas, such as the Ruby Mountain Wilderness Area to the southeast and the Jarbidge Wilderness Area and Wildhorse Reservoir to the north.

For more information, contact the Elko Chamber of Commerce, 1601 Idaho St., Elko, NV 89801, (702) 738-7135.

Nevada's Dazzling Ruby Mountains

THE RUBY MOUNTAINS have a way of making an impression. From the nearest town, which is Elko, you head up a two-lane road, negotiate a curve and then suddenly the Rubies are there — an imposing rock wall dramatically painted on the desert landscape.

The Rubies, located about 20 miles east of Elko, are certainly one of Nevada's most scenic and beautiful mountain ranges. Rising from wide valley floors to peaks of more than 11,000-feet, the Rubies are spectacular representatives of Nevada's famed basin and range topography.

There are two stories about how the mountains were named. One says that the range was named for the ruby garnets that a handful of prospectors claimed they found in the mountains. Apparently, despite the fact that no one ever seemed to be able to produce a single gem found in the mountains, the name stuck.

However, a second story may be closer to the truth. In the late afternoon, when the sun begins to set, the mountains are painted a rich red color. Many locals insist it is this ruby glow that gives the mountains their name — and it's difficult to argue once you've experienced one of these memorable sunsets.

Regardless of the time of year, the Rubies are impressive. In the winter, the mountains, with their deep, rolling contours, resemble a giant, slumbering white caterpillar. Serious skiers can helicopter to the virgin powder found high atop the surrounding peaks, then make their way down the slopes.

In the summer, the mountains become a recreational wonderland with dozens of hiking trails stretching for miles through the rugged country. Hidden in the many canyons and meadows in the range are more than a half-dozen alpine lakes.

The drive through wide Spring Valley goes fast because it's difficult not to stare at the Rubies as you move closer. About three-quarters of the way through the journey you come to a fork in the road with signs indicating the Lamoille Canyon is east and the hamlet of Lamoille is north.

Lamoille is a small cattle and farming community that is the closest to a small midwestern town you'll find in Nevada. It is a lush, fertile community surrounded by fields dotted with cattle or filled with rolled carpets of hay. The Presbyterian Church in Lamoille is all tall steeple and whitewash wood — and somehow reinforces the image that you've stumbled into a rural Minnesota or Wisconsin village.

Lamoille is also noted for several fine restaurants and one of the more downhome bed and breakfasts in the state, the Breitenstein House. Part of a working cattle ranch, the Breitenstein also serves dinner and serves as the headquarters for Ruby Mountain Heli-Skiing, the company that offers helicopter skiing in the Rubies.

The road to Lamoille Canyon is a special treat — although,

keep in mind, it is closed during the winter months due to snow. At the mouth of the canyon, you can stop to enjoy a picnic area alongside a bubbling creek fed by the snowpack.

Farther into the canyon are several overlooks with interpretive signs explaining how the area was carved by glaciers. The view of the surrounding forested glacial canyons is magnificent.

At the end of the 13-½-mile road into the canyon is a parking area and the trailhead for climbing into the mountains. Signs indicate several trails for both long and short hikes. More than 100 miles of hiking trails take you through gorgeous mountain scenery and a handful of beautiful alpine lakes. Hikers can enjoy incredible day trips or find appropriate campsites in the mountains for overnight stays.

In addition to Lamoille Canyon, another scenic trip can be made to the nearby Ruby Marshes. Head back toward Elko from Lamoille Canyon, the turn south on State Route 228. Follow the signs to Jiggs. The road runs parallel to the Rubies and offers a splendid view of the southern part of the range.

A few miles beyond the tiny town of Jiggs (which was actually named for comic-strip character), you'll find the turn-off to Harrison Pass. The route over the pass affords a wonderful view of the mountains from an elevation of more than 7,000 feet as well as the lush Ruby Valley on the southeast side of the range.

On the other side of the pass, you can head south to the Ruby Lake National Wildlife Refuge, also known as the Ruby Marshes. Here, you can fish, boat and camp in an area teeming with wildlife. In the marsh area outside of the refuge, hunting and fishing is popular.

Just south of the marshes is an historic marker commemorating the Pony Express route, which passed through here. The original wooden cabin used by the Pony Express riders was relocated from here to the Northeastern Nevada Museum in Elko, where it has been partially restored.

From the marker, you can head north through some beautiful country to the Ruby Valley School, an historic site, and on to Highway 93, or return to Elko via Harrison Pass.

One of the best reasons for a stop in Elko is a visit to the Northeastern Nevada Museum at 1515 Idaho Street, (702) 738-3418. This fine facility contains exhibits describing the ranching and mining history of the region as well as the natural history, flora and fauna. The museum is open 9 a.m. to 5 p.m., Monday through Saturday, 1-5 p.m. on Sunday. Admission is free, although donations are accepted.

For more information about Elko or the Ruby Mountains, contact the Elko Chamber of Commerce, 1601 Idaho St., Elko, NV 89801, (702) 738-7135.

Ruby Mountains

PART VI

The
Heartland

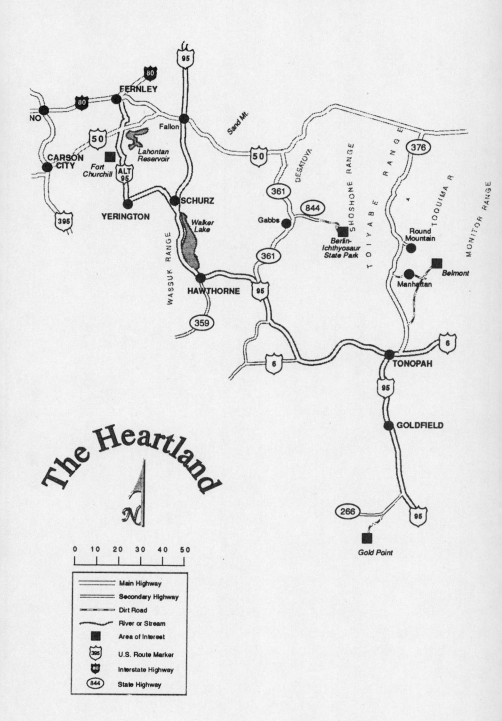

The Heartland

CENTRAL NEVADA is the most misunderstood part of the state. To many people it is a huge, empty chunk of land, best known as the site of the nation's nuclear testing range.

But to others, myself included, this is Nevada's Heartland, a place filled with fascinating mining towns, wild horses and high desert scenery. Nevada's Heartland contains some of the state's most historically important communities, such as Tonopah, Goldfield and Pioche, and many of the best preserved ghost towns in the state.

In the state's earliest days, the center of Nevada was a sparsely populated, somewhat forboding place. The ever-wandering western explorer John C. Fremont crossed through this land in the mid-19th century, glad to have survived. Its first inhabitants were Mormon settlers and itinerant miners.

In the 1860s and 70s, in Belmont, Manhattan and Pioche,

large gold and silver discoveries sparked the development of central Nevada's first significant towns.

The decline of Virginia City in the late 19th century allowed central Nevada to really step to center stage. The discovery of large silver reserves in 1900 prompted the rapid development of Tonopah, followed by equally impressive gold and silver strikes in Goldfield.

Within a few years, most of the political power and a healthy percentage of the population of the state shifted to the Tonopah-Goldfield area. By 1906, Goldfield boasted more than 20,000 residents, dozens of substantial stone and brick buildings, a railroad and the most luxurious hotel in the state.

As with all mining towns, the ore eventually ran out and both Tonopah and Goldfield began rapid declines. As a result of disastrous floods and fire, the latter fell harder and faster than the former, becoming practically a ghost town by the mid-1920s.

Today, central Nevada is home of the greatest concentration of preserved historic mining camps and ghost towns. Places like Tonopah, Goldfield, Berlin, Belmont, Pioche, Gold Point and Rhyolite offer the best opportunity to explore this rich and colorful part of Nevada's history.

Additionally, Nevada's Heartland includes a couple of the state's most important agricultural regions, such as Yerington and the Pahrump Valley (home of the state's only winery), as well as the Hawthorne/Walker Lake area, a true recreational paradise.

Small Town America is Alive and Well in Yerington

IN THE 1870S, there was a saloon in the Mason Valley called the "Willow Switch," that served a homemade whiskey that was so bad, local cowboys called it "poison" or, in the vernacular, "pizen."

It wasn't too long before many buckaroos began to refer to the area as "pizen switch," which was shorthand for "let's go get some pizen down at the switch."

By the mid 1880s, more respectable folks began settling in the area, which was noted for its fertile, green fields. Pizen Switch wasn't exactly a proper name so the residents decided to call their community, Greenfield.

In 1894, community leaders wanted to attract a spur of the Virginia & Truckee Railroad, and changed the name of the town again, this time to honor Henry Marvin Yerington, the railroad's superintendent.

Alas, the V & T chose an alternate route through nearby Wabuska. However, the name stuck and the community of Yerington was born.

Over the years, Yerington has developed into one of Nevada's most important agricultural areas, with local farmers growing quality alfalfa, onions, potatoes and garlic. As a result, a handful of small food-related businesses have cropped up in the area in recent years, including "Sente Me," which makes homemade ravioli and Italian sauces that are available in western Nevada supermarkets.

The best way to reach Yerington, located about an hour-and-a-half from Reno, is to travel south of Carson City on U.S. Highway 395. About an hour from Carson City, take the turnoff to Yerington via Nevada State Route 208.

The road passes through a handful of wide valleys before heading into the picturesque canyons of the East Walker River. Here, steep, rugged rock walls rise above the Walker's rushing waters and along the banks are bushy cottonwoods and lush vegetation. It is lovely, and for a moment, you forget you're in Nevada, the driest state in the union.

After passing out of the canyons, you reach a pair of small farming communities, Wellington and Smith. Both look like things haven't changed a heck of a lot since the 1930s — although the tractors are newer.

Along the way, you pass the Wellington Mercantile, which is located in one of those old barn-shaped buildings that you only see in engravings on the cover of the Farmer's Almanac. It's an old-fashioned general store that sells everything from work shirts to soda pop.

A few miles up the road in Smith, you'll spot white, two-story farmhouses and a one-room, white-washed post office that look like they are straight out of a Norman Rockwell painting — this is the real America. The land around is farming and ranching turf. There are squares of dark, green alfalfa fields alternating with grassy meadows filled with grazing cattle.

It's easy to know when you're getting close to Yerington because you can see a massive mountain of reddish dirt in the distance. The mountain is the remains of tailings scooped from a giant, open-pit copper mine that was the economic mainstay of the region until the late 1970s.

If you drive a little north of the pile, then head west on an unpaved road marked "Weed Heights," you'll find the dwindling remains of a company town that cropped up on the hill overlooking the copper pit. A few dozen folks still live in the rows of box-like houses.

At a spot near the eastern edge of the community, you can park and walk out onto an enclosed deck that affords an impressive view of the copper pit. An unnatural emerald-colored water fills the bottom third of the hole.

Ahead in Yerington, you'll find a picture-perfect representation of an American small town. Walking its main street — called Main Street — is a chance to rediscover what small towns used to be about. Main Street is straight out of a Hollywood backlot with storefronts and a post office that look like they ought to.

The Lyon County Museum on Main Street is one of the best places to learn more about the area's history. Within the museum, you can find displays describing the rise and fall of the area's copper industry, the railroads that once served the region and other area history.

Outside the museum are exhibits that include recreations of a one-room schoolhouse, a barn, a restored blacksmith shop and a general store — and it isn't much different from the one in Wellington.

Yerington also holds an important place in the saga of the American Indian. In 1890, Yerington was the birthplace of the

"Ghost Dance," a brief-lived, but powerful, religious movement that spread through Indian communities across the country.

A Paiute from the Mason Valley area named Wovoka, or the Paiute Messiah, preached a message of spiritual renewal. He said that if his followers performed the "Ghost Dance," the earth would return to the way it was before the arrival of the Europeans.

Unfortunately, Wovoka's basically peaceful teachings were misinterpreted as hostile by some and ultimately led to the death of Sitting Bull, the last great Indian chief.

Wovoka was eventually discredited when his predictions did not come to pass. He returned to a quiet life in Yerington, where he died in 1932. He is buried near the Walker River.

For more information, contact the Mason Valley Chamber of Commerce, Box 327, Yerington, NV 89447, (702) 463-3721.

Yerington School

In Search of Cecil

EVERY LAKE HAS A LEGEND. Scotland's Loch Ness has a monster, Lake Tahoe reportedly has some kind of friendly creature called "Tahoe Tessie" — and Walker Lake, in central Nevada, has "Cecil."

Unlike his colleagues, however, Cecil is quite real. In this case, Cecil is a mechanical sea serpent who once plied the waters of Walker Lake and, in recent years, has been attached to his own trailer for parade appearances.

Cecil, who is the official mascot for Walker Lake and the adjacent community of Hawthorne, is a frequent participant in the annual Nevada Day Parade in Carson City.

Hawthorne, located 150 miles south of Reno via Highway 95, sits just south of Walker Lake. Named in 1881 for local cattleman William Hawthorne, the town was originally a division point for the Carson and Colorado Railroad.

By 1883, Hawthorne had become a regional population center and was designated seat of Esmeralda County (taking it away from the fading mining camp of Aurora).

When Goldfield captured the county seat in 1905, Hawthorne became seat of a new county scooped out of the northern end of Esmeralda County, Mineral County.

The town experienced economic ups and downs during the next few decades, depending on its small, but tenacious, mining industry for survival.

In the 1930s, however, the U.S. Government selected Hawthorne as the site of a new Navy ammunition dump. During World War II, the town ballooned to more than 13,000 residents. The population dropped again following the war, but there has been a fairly stable military presence in the area over the years.

The military continues to be important to Hawthorne. In fact, one of the prettiest short drives is through the shaded military base. To do this, you must drive to the main entrance and tell the guard you want to see the golf course.

Once inside, visitors can see fine examples of the sturdy, red brick military housing popular during the 1930s. There is also an excellent golf course, one of the best-groomed in rural Nevada.

There are other interesting places in the area. The Mineral County Museum at 10th and D Streets features some nice exhibits about the area's history.

In the center of town is Joe's Tavern, one of those ancient, cluttered saloons with walls that offer an eclectic view of Nevada history with vintage campaign photos and signs, antiques and old firearms.

Walker Lake is a paradise for water sports enthusiasts. The lake is popular for fishing (particularly in the fall and winter), boating and swimming. Picnic tables are located along U.S. Highway 95 at Tamarack Point and Sportsmen's Beach.

Walker Lake is home of the annual Walker Lake 100 speed-boat race and several fishing derbies.

Just north of the lake is Schurz, a small, quiet community that was once an Indian school. The town is part of the Walker Lake Indian Reservation and home of the annual Pinenut Festival, a celebration of the local native American culture held each September.

Hawthorne is also central to a number of Nevada ghost towns including Rawhide (40 miles north), Marietta (35 miles southwest), Candelaria (40 miles southwest) and Aurora.

The latter is located twenty-seven miles southwest of Hawthorne via Nevada State Route 359 and a marked dirt road. This former mining camp is one of the state's most mistreated ghost towns.

Aurora was founded in 1860 by prospectors searching for water and game. By the following year, Aurora had grown large enough to be named seat of two counties — Mono in California and Esmeralda in Nevada.

By 1863, more than 10,000 people had moved to Aurora, which was finally placed in Nevada. (There had been a dispute over the location of the state line, hence its status as county seat in two states.)

The next year, however, the mines began to play out and by the 1880s, Hawthorne has taken away the county seat.

Aurora began to disappear after the last of its mines closed in 1919. Vandals and the elements damaged many of the buildings and then, during the 1940s, the town's brick buildings were torn down so the materials could be reused.

Visitors won't find much remaining in Aurora except foundations of the former buildings.

A few miles from Aurora, in California, is Bodie, another former mining camp that is one of the west's best-preserved ghost towns. Bodie was founded in about 1859 and within two decades had grown to more than ten thousand residents. The town began to decline in the early part of this century and was largely abandoned by 1962 when the California Department of Parks and Recreation acquired it for preservation.

Visitors, today, will find a fairly extensive series of buildings and remains of old Bodie. Dozens of structures, ranging from homes to businesses still stand. Despite the seemingly large number of preserved structures, present-day Bodie represents only about 5 percent of the town at its peak.

Guided tours are offered at 10 a.m. and 3 p.m. daily. The park is best visited during the summer months when the road is dry. The park is open year-round, 9 a.m. to 7 p.m. in the summer and 9 a.m. to 4 p.m. the rest of the year.

For more information about Hawthorne, contact the Mineral County Chamber of Commerce, Box 1635, Hawthorne, NV 89415, (702) 945-5896. For information about Bodie, contact the Bodie State Historic Park, P.O. Box 515, Bridgeport, CA 93517, (619) 647-6445.

Walker Lake

Tonopah's Silver Trails

JIM BUTLER might have made a good television minister or auditor for the Pentagon — some job that wasn't too challenging.

Butler was the man who discovered the Tonopah area's rich silver deposits, then proceeded to work his claim as little as possible.

In fact, Butler became a millionaire by allowing others to work his claim in return for a cut.

Legend has it that in 1900, Butler, a sometime miner, camped at the area called Tonopah by the local Paiute tribe. (The word means "brush water" because of the presence of springs in the area.)

His burro wandered off during a windstorm. Butler found the animal huddled under an outcropping, which contained some intriguing rocks. He chipped a few samples for later analysis. (He was so nonchalant about his discovery that it was several months before he got around to finding out what he had discovered.)

The rocks proved to contain incredibly rich amounts of silver and the Tonopah rush was on.

Within two years, Tonopah was a thriving community with 3,000 residents, two newspapers, more than two dozen saloons and a couple of churches.

By 1905, it succeeded in acquiring the county seat from faltering Belmont.

Tonopah's discovery, as well as the major strikes in nearby Goldfield, proved to be a much needed shot in the arm for Nevada's mining industry which had bottomed following the end of the Comstock boom in Virginia City.

Today, Tonopah is one of the best places to find the authentic feel of life in a turn-of-the-century Nevada mining camp. Tonopah is located 228 miles south of Carson City via Highway 50 (to Silver Springs), then south on Highway 95.

The reminders of the area's rich mining history are everywhere. Tonopah's hillsides are still littered with the remains of mining operations.

The old downtown has a number of the town's original buildings, such as the Mizpah Hotel. Built in 1907 on the site of one of Jim Butler's original mining discoveries, the Mizpah is a grand five-story building.

The hotel was restored in 1979 and is worth a stroll through. Sit at the classic bar and imagine that the legendary Jack Dempsey once worked there as a bouncer.

Tonopah's Central Nevada Historical Museum, located on Tonopah's main street just southeast of the downtown is probably the best place to learn about the area's history.

The museum contains good displays about Tonopah's mines, the railroads that once served the area, life in Tonopah at the turn of the century and the military's presence in the region.

Mizpah Hotel, Tonopah

Outside the museum building are fine examples of historic mining equipment.

With its services, hotels and motels, Tonopah is also an excellent spot to stay while exploring some of the ghost towns that can be found in the area. Be aware that there are few services outside Tonopah.

Additionally, one of the best ghost towns in the state is Belmont, located 47 miles northeast of Tonopah via Highway 6 and Nevada Route 376 and 82.

As you reach Belmont (note that the last four miles are maintained and graded dirt road), one of the first things you notice is the Belmont-Monitor off to the left of the main road. To the right is the Belmont Cemetery, a fine frontier graveyard that has been well maintained over the years.

Ahead, is the downtown which still boasts the remains of a number of historic buildings, such as the first story of the Cosmopolitan Saloon and the picturesque red brick facade of an old bank.

To the north is the famous Belmont courthouse, part of the Nevada State Park system. The courthouse was built in 1867 and was used until about 1905, when Tonopah became the county seat. It has been partially restored, but awaits funding for the remainder of the work, such as the interior.

If you follow the main road through Belmont's downtown, then continue south over a ridge that rises above the community, you will spot other ruins of homes and businesses. About a mile south are the impressive ruins of another stamp mill and the massive smoke stack of an old brick factory that rises high above the nearby Monitor Valley.

For more information, contact the Tonopah Chamber of Commerce, Box 869, Tonopah, NV 89049, (702) 482-3558 or the Central Nevada Museum, 482-9676.

Goldfield's Treasures
on Display

A PHOTOGRAPH hanging in an old antique store tells the story.

The scene is a rooftop view of Goldfield about 85 years ago. The scene shows dozens of blocks of two and three-story brick buildings seemingly surrounded by acres of houses and other wooden structures.

It is Goldfield in its glory, when this community nestled in the shadows of Columbia Mountain was the largest and most powerful city in Nevada.

In 1902, silver and gold were discovered near Goldfield, which is located about halfway between Reno and Las Vegas on U.S. Highway 95.

Within a few years, the city literally exploded with growth. Within its first decade, Goldfield acquired more than 25,000 residents, dozens of saloons, a couple of banks, a railroad, a magnificent courthouse and the most fabulous hotel between Kansas City and San Francisco.

From 1905 to 1910, Goldfield evolved into the center of business, commerce and political might in Nevada. It created mining millionaires and power-brokers who would rule the state for years to come, although, it turned out, not necessarily from Goldfield.

In 1906, Goldfield truly came of age, hosting the world lightweight boxing championship fight between Joe Gans and "Battlin' Nelson."

But the ride on this mining cart was to be short. By 1911, the ore became harder to find and the town had already started its decline. In September 1913, the first serious blow to the community's future was struck when a flashflood washed away several blocks of homes.

By the time the second great disaster occurred — a tremendous fire in 1923 that destroyed 53 square blocks of buildings — Goldfield was already becoming a ghost town.

Wandering the dusty streets of Goldfield today, it's difficult to imagine how big this town must have been eight-and-a-half decades ago. Still, there is enough of the community remaining to allow you to appreciate what is certainly one of the most fascinating of Nevada's great mining camps.

Walking the streets of Goldfield is like turning the pages of an old picture album. Because it was such a substantial community, the streets are dotted with intriguing historic buildings and ruins, including the massive Goldfield Hotel.

Completed in 1908, the four-story hotel was the best of its day. It boasted a solid mahogany lobby, crystal chandeliers and one of the first Otis elevators west of the Mississippi.

The hotel, like the city, began a gradual decline during the 1920s and, by the 1930s, had become a flop house for cowboys and undiscriminating travelers. It finally closed its doors in the 1940s, after having been used to quarter soldiers during WW II.

Over the years, many local people have struggled to save the hotel from falling into total disrepair. Most recently, a San Francisco investor purchased the old hotel and began restoring it, but did not complete the job before running out of money. It still awaits a buyer to complete the job.

Other buildings offer further glimpses into Goldfield's past. For instance, the impressive brick Goldfield High School, across the street from the County Courthouse, is a classic example of the kind of early 20th century architecture found in Nevada mining towns, despite its ramshackle appearance.

No visitor to Goldfield should forget to stop for a refreshment at one of the town's three old-time western saloons. The Santa Fe Saloon is the oldest in Goldfield and is the most colorful with its original oak backbar, wooden sidewalk and slightly warped wooden floorboards.

The bar opened in 1905 — making it also one of the oldest in the state — and is located north of the main section of town at the entrance to the mining fields at the base of Columbia Mountain.

Equally unique are the Mozart Saloon, located across the highway from the Goldfield Hotel and the Green Parrot Saloon at the south end of town. The latter is noted for its bar counter which is covered by more than 150,000 pennies.

You can make an interesting drive through the old mining fields. Massive metal and wooden head frames seem to grow in the stark, barren foothills north of the town. If you decide to take a look be extremely careful, because many of the old mine shafts are open.

Another landmark in Goldfield is the former Tex Rickard home, across the street from the courthouse. This quaint Victorian was built on the corner of Crook and Franklin streets in 1906 by Rickard, who was, at the time, a local saloon owner.

Rickard was the mastermind behind the famous Nelson-Gans fight. In fact, his experience with that event helped catapult him into the ranks of the major boxing promoters. He would ultimately gain fame as the man who built the original Madison Square Garden in New York City.

The Esmeralda County Courthouse on Highway 95 is one of the most unique buildings in town. Built of native sandstone and resembling a castle, the courthouse was one of the most elaborate in the state when built. Inside one of the courtrooms, you will find original Tiffany lamps.

Every lot and building in Goldfield seems to have a story and one of the best ways to learn more is with the help of someone local. One of the most helpful is Virginia Ridgeway, owner of the Gloryhole Antique shop, and a walking encyclopedia of information about Goldfield. Visitors should feel free to stop by her store, located across the street from the Goldfield Hotel, to ask about the town.

For more information, contact the Goldfield Chamber of Commerce, Box 225, Goldfield, NV 89013, (702) 485-9957.

Goldfield

The Resurrection
of Gold Point

IT'S NOT OFTEN that you hear about a ghost town being brought back to life.

Herb Robbins, however, has this crazy dream that someday the ghost town of Gold Point in central Nevada will become one of the state's living ghost towns, like Virginia City.

Gold Point is located about 35 miles southwest of Goldfield via U.S. Highway 95 and Nevada State Route 266.

"I started buying up land in Gold Point in 1979," Robbins recalled. "In the beginning, it was just a place to go. I bought three lots and would go out and spend a night in a tent."

After more than a decade of acquiring land, Robbins, who works as a wallpaper hanger in Los Angeles during most of the year, is part owner of most of the buildings and about half of the land in Gold Point.

The bearded, soft-spoken Robbins, who calls himself the

"Mayor of Gold Point," purchased the former post office and several other buildings, then began to tedious task of restoring and maintaining the dilapidated wooden storefronts and mining shacks. He estimates that he and partner Walt Kremin have invested more than $150,000 in their dream.

"I have to go hang wallpaper to support my habit out there," he joked.

Robbins, who is 38, said that he plans to continue his restoration efforts and would like to eventually relocate to his ghost town.

"I want a bed and breakfast and I plan to sell gasoline and have the bar," he said. "I really feel that once I'm there full-time, it'll really take off. This is where I want to retire and live when I'm old and gray."

In addition to his house, he has restored and enlarged the post office into a cozy saloon, complete with tabletop shuffleboard and pool table. Next door, he has a small museum filled with objects and antiques he's found throughout the town and collected over the years.

He is also beginning work on public bathrooms and a two-story addition to the saloon that will include rooms and a kitchen.

And, for the last couple of years, he has sponsored a large celebration, called Wiley Days, during the July 4 weekend. Several hundred people have attended the four day event, which includes a fireworks show.

Robbins said that the event is named for Nevada State Senator Harry Wiley and his wife, Ora May, who were among the town's founders and residents for more than 50 years.

History books indicate that Gold Point was originally known as Lime Point in honor of lime deposits discovered there in 1868. The area was only sporadically mined until the early 1880s when silver was discovered. The high cost of transporting the

Gold Point

ore, however, led to it being abandoned again a few years later.

In 1905, the Great Western mine opened and the area became active once more. The discovery of high-grade ore in 1908 sparked a boom and a new name for the town, Hornsilver, after the type of silver ore that was found there.

Eventually more than 200 buildings were erected in the mining town, which also boasted a newspaper, the Hornsilver Herald. Mining continued for more than two decades and the name of the town was changed to Gold Point in 1930 to reflect that more gold than silver was being produced.

The mines were finally closed in 1942, when most of the workers were called to serve during World War II. The town began a rapid decline, and by the 1950s was largely abandoned.

A walk around Gold Point is an opportunity to catch a glimpse of Nevada's past. Across from the post office saloon and museum on the dusty main street, are a neat row of tiny, one and two-room wooden miner's shacks, while several impressive headframes stand silent on the hillsides outside of the town.

At the Townsite Mine just south of town the thick red-colored headframe timbers are worn and dried by the seemingly constant winds that whip down from the surrounding hills into the flat town area.

A rusted wire mesh covering on a mine shaft hints at the hidden depths where men toiled in the dark for a few bucks a day.

"I want to save this town so people can see what other generations were like," Robbins said. "There are numerous stories of how these towns disappear. I won't let that happen to Gold Point."

Berlin's Ghosts and Big Fish

IMAGINE THE UNUSUAL combination of an historic ghost town and an archaeological dig site and you've got the Berlin-Ichthyosaur State Park located near Gabbs.

Within the confines of the same park, you can stroll through the aging remains of a turn-of-the-century mining ghost town, then, only a short drive away, find the remains of giant fish dinosaurs that thrived in Nevada about 150 million years ago.

Berlin-Ichthyosaur State Park is 150 miles east of Reno via Interstate 80 and U.S. Highway 50 through Fernley. At Middle Gate (located about 40 miles east of Fallon), turn south on State Route 361 to Gabbs. Before you reach Gabbs, turn east and follow the signs to the park. The last six miles is a maintained gravel road.

Berlin was one of the later mining discoveries during Nevada's silver age. Precious silver was uncovered in 1895 and within three years, a large stamp mill had been erected using equipment taken from nearby Ione, where silver had been discovered earlier.

In a short time, a town began to form, and by 1905 Berlin could boast about 250 residents, a general store, a post office, an auto repair shop, an assay office, three saloons, a school house and a stage line that connected the isolated community to other mining camps.

However, like most Nevada mining towns, the early promise suggested by the quality of the ore proved to be illusionary at Berlin's mines. By 1909, the mill was closed and the people had begun to move on to more productive locations. During the following decade, the tailings (piles of the remains of rock taken from the mines) were actively reworked to squeeze out every particle of valuable ore.

The mill was finally stripped of its contents during World War II, when it became valuable as scrap metal. During the next few decades, Berlin stood empty. A mining company caretaker continued to protect the buildings, but the only other inhabitants were those souls forgotten in the town's cemetery.

In the 1970s, the town was acquired by the Nevada State Park system, which has gradually repaired the aging buildings, maintaining them in what is termed a "state of arrested decay."

Today, during the summer months, the park rangers will take you on a tour of Berlin. The impressive mill building is still standing, behind it an ore cart trellis leads to the mines on the nearby hill. Other buildings have also been saved, including the old assay office and several miner's homes. The remains of a corral can be found by searching for ground littered with glass shards; apparently the ranch hands would often shoot glass bottles off the barn fence.

The ichthyosaur dig site is equally interesting. Ichthyosaurs (the word means "fish lizards") once swam in the massive ocean

Berlin-Ichthyosaur State Park

that covered what is now western Nevada. The reptiles resided in the area from 185 million years ago and became extinct about 70 million years ago.

For reasons unknown, about 34 of these giant prehistoric fish became beached in the Union Canyon near Berlin. During the informative tour available at the site, the ranger speculates that the ichthyosaurs, like modern-day pilot whales, may have beached themselves in a group. Other evidence suggests they were trapped, one by one, along a muddy shore by the receding tide.

The giant reptiles died on the beach, their bodies were covered by the mud and sand. Geologists estimate that 3,000 feet of mud eventually piled on the bones. The soft ooze hardened, and the bones were petrified over millions of years.

The site was discovered in the 1930s by paleontologists and, to date, has yielded the largest and best examples of ichthyosaur bones ever found. Since then, it has been the site of several major digs.

A large sculpture wall near the enclosed dig site displays a full ichthyosaur, and gives visitors some idea of the size of these big fish.

Berlin-Ichthyosaur Park also has some fourteen campsites with picnic tables, barbecue grills and water. The remoteness provides for a quiet vacation spot far from bright lights and traffic.

For more information, contact the Nevada Division of State Parks, Capitol Complex, Carson City, NV 89710, (702) 687-4387.

Respecting Nevada's Disappearing Ghost Towns

Off the beaten track, at the end of those unmarked dirt roads that are forever branching off from the main highways, 100 ghost towns dot the Nevada landscape. A collapsing hulk of a stone building, a scattering of brownboard shacks defeated by time and abandonment, the barely discernible remnant of a wide main street, a nearby hillside riddled with the black apertures of mine tunnels and littered with mounds of discarded rock, and the moaning of the desert wind in the encompassing silence are all that remain of the boom-and-bust towns that flourished and died in the wreckage of broken dreams.

— Nevada author Bob Laxalt

ONE OF NEVADA'S richest resources is its history. While the state is relatively young compared to places like Rhode Island or Massachusetts, it was founded during a time and in a place that has long captured the imagination.

Nevada is the Old West of cowboys, Indians, outlaws and sourdoughs. It was the original field of dreams; a place where fortunes were created from green stones, blue mud and miles of hard gray rock.

The state boasted the richest silver and gold strikes in the world, the West's first train robbery and last stagecoach hold-up.

Because so many of Nevada's towns grew up around mining discoveries, there has long been a cycle of boom-and-bust in the state's economy. Indeed, Nevada reportedly has more than five ghost towns for every living town.

There is a special feeling — call it the feel of tangible history — when discovering, then exploring a Nevada ghost town. Walking the dirt streets of a once-thriving community allows you to play amateur historian and detective as you speculate on the story behind each structure and foundation.

Few of the remaining ghost towns are located near population centers, which is perhaps for the best, given the sorry history of how these historic sites have been treated over the years.

There are plenty of examples of people's casual attitude about Nevada's history. Author David Toll tells the tale of the fate of one such town, Aurora, in his excellent book, *The Compleat Nevada Traveler.*

Aurora, located about 25 miles southwest of Hawthorne, boomed in the 1860s and 1870s, then gradually faded by the end of the century. A substantial community with many brick buildings, Aurora was dismantled in the late 1940s by a developer who sold the materials on the used brick market. Today, only foundations remain.

Despite generally poor treatment, one can still find glimpses of formerly substantial communities half-hidden in high canyons and valleys throughout the state.

Belmont

Belmont, located 47 miles northeast of Tonopah via U.S. Highway 6 and Nevada State routes 376 and 82, remains one of the better examples of a 19th century Nevada mining camp.

While not a true ghost town — a handful of people live there — it is probably because of the presence of residents that more of the town has not been destroyed.

The residents are protective. Don't be surprised if someone walks out to ask your business when you visit Belmont. As with any fragile historic resource, look, but don't touch.

About 49 miles north of Tonopah via U.S. Highway 6 and Nevada State routes 376 and 377 is Manhattan, another former mining town that provides a look at Nevada's mining past and present.

The past is represented by several historic buildings such as the photogenic Manhattan Catholic Church, built in the 1870s. This classic frontier chapel was originally located in Belmont, then moved to Manhattan at the turn of the century.

The present can be seen in the massive open pit mining operations in the Manhattan area. The region remains a major producer of gold in the state.

In fact, one of the intriguing things about visiting Manhattan is observing the modern mining operations adjacent to the aging wooden headframes and stamp mill ruins on the surrounding hillsides.

For more information about Nevada's ghost towns, pick up a copy of Stanley Paher's *Nevada Ghost Towns and Mining Camps*, considered by many, including me, to be the Bible when it comes to exploring ghost towns.